T0209670

An Analysis of

Judith Butler's

Gender Trouble

Tim Smith-Laing

Published by Macat International Ltd
24:13 Coda Centre, 189 Munster Road, London SW6 6AW.

Distributed exclusively by Routledge
2 Park Square, Milton Park, Abingdon, Oxon OX14 4RN
711 Third Avenue, New York, NY 10017, USA

Routledge is an imprint of the Taylor & Francis Group, an informa business

www.macat.com
info@macat.com

Cataloguing in Publication Data
A catalogue record for this book is available from the British Library.
Library of Congress Cataloguing-in-Publication Data is available upon request.
Cover illustration: Etienne Gilfillan

ISBN 978-1-912302-83-3 (hardback)
ISBN 978-1-912127-76-4 (paperback)
ISBN 978-1-912281-71-8 (e-book)

Notice
The information in this book is designed to orientate readers of the work under analysis,
to elucidate and contextualise its key ideas and themes, and to aid in the development
of critical thinking skills. It is not meant to be used, nor should it be used, as a
substitute for original thinking or in place of original writing or research. References and
notes are provided for informational purposes and their presence does not constitute
endorsement of the information or opinions therein. This book is presented solely for
educational purposes. It is sold on the understanding that the publisher is not engaged
to provide any scholarly advice. The publisher has made every effort to ensure that
this book is accurate and up-to-date, but makes no warranties or representations with
regard to the completeness or reliability of the information it contains. The information
and the opinions provided herein are not guaranteed or warranted to produce particular
results and may not be suitable for students of every ability. The publisher shall not be
liable for any loss, damage or disruption arising from any errors or omissions, or from
the use of this book, including, but not limited to, special, incidental, consequential or
other damages caused, or alleged to have been caused, directly or indirectly, by the
information contained within.

CONTENTS

THE MACAT LIBRARY

The Macat Library is a series of unique academic explorations of seminal works in the humanities and social sciences – books and papers that have had a significant and widely recognised impact on their disciplines. It has been created to serve as much more than just a summary of what lies between the covers of a great book. It illuminates and explores the influences on, ideas of, and impact of that book. Our goal is to offer a learning resource that encourages critical thinking and fosters a better, deeper understanding of important ideas.

Each publication is divided into three Sections: Influences, Ideas, and Impact. Each Section has four Modules. These explore every important facet of the work, and the responses to it.

This Section-Module structure makes a Macat Library book easy to use, but it has another important feature. Because each Macat book is written to the same format, it is possible (and encouraged!) to cross-reference multiple Macat books along the same lines of inquiry or research. This allows the reader to open up interesting interdisciplinary pathways.

To further aid your reading, lists of glossary terms and people mentioned are included at the end of this book (these are indicated by an asterisk [*] throughout) – as well as a list of works cited.

Macat has worked with the University of Cambridge to identify the elements of critical thinking and understand the ways in which six different skills combine to enable effective thinking.
Three allow us to fully understand a problem; three more give us the tools to solve it. Together, these six skills make up the **PACIER** model of critical thinking. They are:

ANALYSIS – understanding how an argument is built
EVALUATION – exploring the strengths and weaknesses of an argument
INTERPRETATION – understanding issues of meaning

CREATIVE THINKING – coming up with new ideas and fresh connections
PROBLEM-SOLVING – producing strong solutions
REASONING – creating strong arguments

To find out more, visit **WWW.MACAT.COM.**

CRITICAL THINKING AND *GENDER TROUBLE*

Primary critical thinking skill: CREATIVE THINKING
Secondary critical thinking skill: INTERPRETATION

Judith Butler's *Gender Trouble* is a perfect example of creative thinking. The book redefines feminism's struggle against patriarchy as part of a much broader issue: the damaging effects of all our assumptions about gender and identity.

Looking at the factionalism of contemporary (1980s) feminism, Butler saw a movement split by identity politics. Riven by arguments over what it meant to be a women, over sexuality, and over class and race, feminism was falling prey to internal problems of identity, and was failing to move towards broader solidarity with other liberation movements such as LGBT.

Butler turned these issues on their head by questioning the basis that supposedly fundamental and fixed identities such as 'masculine/feminine' or 'straight/gay' actually have. Tracing these binary definitions back to the binary nature of human anatomy ('male/female'), she argues that there is no necessary link between our anatomies and our identities. Subjecting a wide range of evidence from philosophy, cultural theory, anthropology, psychology and anthropology to a renewed search for meaning, Butler shows both that sex (biology) and gender (identity) are separate, and that even biological sex is not simplistically either/or male/female. Separating our biology from identity then allows her to argue that, while categories such as 'masculine/feminine/straight/gay' are real, they are not necessary; rather, they are the product of society's assumptions, and the constant reproduction of those assumptions by everyone around us. That opens up some small hope for change: a hope that – 25 years after *Gender Trouble*'s publication – is having a huge impact on societies and politics across the world.

ABOUT THE AUTHOR OF THE ORIGINAL WORK

American philosopher and gender theorist **Judith Butler** was born in Ohio in 1956. She is now a distinguished professor in California and Switzerland. Her concern with how society creates outcasts is rooted in her own life: relatives were murdered in the Nazi concentration camps, a transsexual uncle lived in an institution, and her own coming out as a lesbian at 16 was "tempestuous."
Butler virtually invented queer theory, but, while *Gender Trouble* made her famous, today she is equally controversial for her views on Israel.

ABOUT THE AUTHOR OF THE ANALYSIS

Dr Tim Smith-Laing took his DPhil in English literature at Merton College, Oxford, and has held positions at Jesus College, Oxford, and Sciences Po in Paris.

ABOUT MACAT

GREAT WORKS FOR CRITICAL THINKING

Macat is focused on making the ideas of the world's great thinkers accessible and comprehensible to everybody, everywhere, in ways that promote the development of enhanced critical thinking skills.

It works with leading academics from the world's top universities to produce new analyses that focus on the ideas and the impact of the most influential works ever written across a wide variety of academic disciplines. Each of the works that sit at the heart of its growing library is an enduring example of great thinking. But by setting them in context – and looking at the influences that shaped their authors, as well as the responses they provoked – Macat encourages readers to look at these classics and game-changers with fresh eyes. Readers learn to think, engage and challenge their ideas, rather than simply accepting them.

'Macat offers an amazing first-of-its-kind tool for interdisciplinary learning and research. Its focus on works that transformed their disciplines and its rigorous approach, drawing on the world's leading experts and educational institutions, opens up a world-class education to anyone.'

Andreas Schleicher
Director for Education and Skills, Organisation for Economic
Co-operation and Development

'Macat is taking on some of the major challenges in university education ... They have drawn together a strong team of active academics who are producing teaching materials that are novel in the breadth of their approach.'

Prof Lord Broers,
former Vice-Chancellor of the University of Cambridge

'The Macat vision is exceptionally exciting. It focuses upon new modes of learning which analyse and explain seminal texts which have profoundly influenced world thinking and so social and economic development. It promotes the kind of critical thinking which is essential for any society and economy. This is the learning of the future.'

Rt Hon Charles Clarke, former UK Secretary of State for Education

'The Macat analyses provide immediate access to the critical conversation surrounding the books that have shaped their respective discipline, which will make them an invaluable resource to all of those, students and teachers, working in the field.'

Professor William Tronzo, University of California at San Diego

WAYS IN TO THE TEXT

KEY POINTS

- Judith Butler is an American feminist* philosopher whose landmark 1990 book revolutionized thinking about sex* (the biological differences between people commonly used to distinguish us as "male" or "female"), sexuality* (the specific nature of our sexual desires), and gender* (roughly, the behaviors commonly used to distinguish "female" and "male").

- *Gender Trouble: Feminism and the Subversion of Identity* argues that gender identity is not natural,* but a product of social convention—an "act" that becomes true.

- Butler transformed how gender is studied and understood in philosophy literature, and also how certain groups set about demanding political change.

Who Is Judith Butler?

Judith Butler, the author of *Gender Trouble* (1990), is an American philosopher who was born in Cleveland, Ohio, in 1956. She attended a Jewish school until she was 18 and was so fascinated by the origin and nature of ideas that she received extra lessons in ethics* and philosophy. At the age of 16, she came out as a lesbian.

Butler went to Bennington College (a private seat of learning in the state of Vermont) and then studied for her PhD in philosophy at

Yale University, where she became a prominent member of the lesbian community and a political activist. She received her doctorate in 1984 and now teaches at the University of California, Berkeley, and in Switzerland.

A feminist (that is, a participant in the cultural, political, and theoretical currents surrounding the advocacy of the rights of women), she has published more than a dozen books and has been active in debates ranging from lesbian, gay, bisexual, and transsexual rights to Middle Eastern politics. She works on identity issues and prejudice against minorities, having personal experience of both. Her mother lost her Hungarian family in the Nazi Holocaust* during World War II, and, as a lesbian, Butler has herself experienced discrimination. She has spoken about the difficulty of coming out as a teenager and about the scars she has received on account of her sexuality. Her uncle was confined to a medical institution for his "anatomically anomalous body,"[1] and this also influenced Butler's thinking about the pressure to conform to society in accepted ways.

Through *Gender Trouble*, Butler became a celebrity with a worldwide readership and at least one fanzine.* Since the early 2000s she has entered another controversial debate, becoming an outspoken critic of Israeli state policies on terrorism and Palestine, the geographical region that includes Israel, the West Bank and the Gaza Strip.

What Does *Gender Trouble* Say?

Gender Trouble: Feminism and the Subversion of Identity argues that people must rethink the most basic categories of human identity to make society better. Butler achieves this by asking skeptical questions about sex, gender, and sexuality, and how these define people's identities. Why do we label ourselves and others as "straight" or "gay," or even as "male" or "female"? Where do these categories come from? How do they contribute to prejudice in society? How can questioning these labels help change society?

For Butler, assumptions about what is "normal" result in "non-normal" people having less fulfilling lives. With gender identities it is viewed as "normal" for men to behave in masculine ways and women in feminine ways. Men who behave in feminine ways or women who behave in masculine ways are considered abnormal or strange. They suffer prejudice, ranging from simple stares in the street to actual violence against them; this negatively affects their lives. While homosexuality* (a sexual preference for someone of the same sex) is commonly accepted today in law and general society, society still tends to view heterosexuality* as "normal." This leaves other sexualities labeled as "abnormal." Even where open prejudice does not exist, this labeling has a negative effect on the lives of those identifying with these sexualities.

Butler asks why this should be so. Where do these categories of normal come from, and what makes them so strong? Is there, for instance, any necessary or natural link between being a man and being masculine? If not, why does there seem to be one? What if there is no necessary link between biological sex (being a man or woman) and gender (behaving in masculine or feminine ways)? Why should it be considered normal for men to be attracted to women rather than to men?

Butler's central argument is that there is no natural basis to gender, and no inherent link between gender and someone's sex. Instead, social conventions about dress and behavior give the appearance of a natural basis. This makes it seem as though masculine behavior is "natural" for men. Butler sees this understanding of naturalness as coming from society as a whole. It comes from everybody's actions. It is people acting in certain expected ways that makes gender "real." Men and women acting as expected makes masculinity and femininity exist. Butler terms this process "performative,"* a complex term that is key to her work.

The performative is not just a performance; it is a performance that makes itself real. Knowing that this is the case, though, can help people change the script.

Gender Trouble has sold over 100,000 copies and been published in 13 languages. It is widely considered the most influential text in the history of gender studies, and has had an impact on a broad range of disciplines. Famously considered a founding text of queer theory* (roughly, the study of what we mean by "normal" when we discuss matters of sexuality and identity), it has become a key text in the history of feminism and lesbian, gay, bisexual,* and transgender* rights—as well as in philosophy and literary criticism. By forcing readers to think again about the fundamental identity categories of the modern world, *Gender Trouble* sparked a series of debates that continue to the present day.

Why Does *Gender Trouble* Matter?

It is impossible to exaggerate the importance of *Gender Trouble* for anyone interested in philosophy or culture theory. From the moment it appeared in 1990, it was hailed as a pivotal text in the history of feminism. Since then it has become one of the most referenced books in modern philosophy, and one of the most significant texts in the history of culture theory.

This reputation shows no sign of fading, because *Gender Trouble* has revolutionized critical writing across the academic world. In literature it transformed discussions of gender and sexuality, from the classics to the present day. In feminism it challenged the very idea of "women." In philosophy it created a new language for tackling identity. In cultural studies it changed the way critics read the world.

Mastering the vocabulary Butler uses in *Gender Trouble* is useful to any student discussing sex, sexuality, or gender. In fact, that vocabulary is vital to anyone discussing individual identity—in politics, the academic world, or daily life. Even its title has become a common phrase in literary criticism. *Gender Trouble* provides useful tools for any student in the humanities because Butler uses philosophy, psychoanalysis,* literature, and biology to make her case.

Butler's ideas about gender, sexuality, and identity have changed the way critics consider texts. *Gender Trouble* brought about a rethinking of everything, ranging from the conventions of heroes and lovers, to the complex ways in which books belong to their times. Even when critics are not directly quoting Butler, they are often using her ideas.

Getting to grips with *Gender Trouble* is a rewarding challenge. Densely written and technical, it is difficult to understand without hard work and guidance. It also forces readers to rethink the ideas they have held all their lives—ideas they have taken for granted as the basic "facts of life." Although *Gender Trouble* has caused countless arguments among academics, activists, and general readers, it is one of a small number of texts that can claim to change the way readers see the world.

Butler's big questions are all the more urgent as we grapple with new issues around the roles and rights of women and people of all sexualities in different countries and across cultures. Understanding how the "correct" gender rules are imposed by society requires a top-to-bottom rethink of what it is to be male or female, masculine or feminine, straight, bisexual, lesbian, gay, or transgender—what, in other words, it means to be human.

NOTES

1   Judith Butler, *Gender Trouble: Feminism and the Subversion of Identity* (Abingdon: Routledge, 1999).

SECTION 1
INFLUENCES

THE AUTHOR AND THE HISTORICAL CONTEXT

KEY POINTS

- *Gender Trouble* changed forever how feminist* and queer studies* scholars discussed gender.*

- Judith Butler's ideas grew from her dislike of the rules about identity laid down first by her Jewish community when she was growing up, and then by the lesbian-feminist community of which she was a part at university.

- Butler was writing in the late 1980s, when feminist and homosexual* activism also adopted an oppressive attitude to identity.

Why Read this Text?

Gender Trouble: Feminism and the Subversion of Identity made Judith Butler an instant celebrity when it was published in 1990—and she remains one of the most famous philosophers in the world. The book caused a great stir in feminist philosophy and politics, and while some reviewers struggled with its "dense, complexifying style,"[1] others called it "indispensable" reading.[2]

Gender Trouble set out startling new ideas about gender by arguing that it is a "performative"* creation. In other words, she claimed that being "masculine" or "feminine" involves a process of acting as one or the other, but that a person's biological sex* (male/female) is not necessarily linked to the gender (masculine/feminine) they "perform." *Performative* is more than a mere *performance* though, because behaving a certain way makes that way real. So gender is not just a matter of people copying it by acting in a certain way; it is actually *produced* by them acting in a certain way.

> **❝** I began to be interested in philosophy when I was 14, and I was in trouble in the synagogue. The rabbi said, 'You are too talkative in class. You talk back, you are not well behaved. You have to come and have a tutorial with me.' I said 'OK, great!' I was thrilled. **❞**
>
> Judith Butler, 2010 interview, *Haaretz*

Butler sets out the even more radical idea that biological sex is itself a product of cultural assumptions. She asks why we only see two sexes when nature presents a whole spectrum of bodies between the two poles of male and female.

These ideas caused a revolution in the discussion of gender across academia. Most famously, *Gender Trouble* was instrumental in the foundation of queer theory,* (inquiry into the unstable nature of categorization, often in issues surrounding sexuality and identity) and it has been a major influence on political thinkers and activists since the 1990s, especially within feminism. As the literary theorist Gayatri Chakravorty Spivak* predicted, *Gender Trouble* is now a fixture of undergraduate courses in women's studies.[3]

Author's Life
Butler was born on February 24, 1956, in Cleveland, Ohio, into an American Jewish family of Hungarian and Russian descent. She attended Hebrew school as a child and by the time she was a teenager was fascinated by Jewish ethics* and philosophy. She was also profoundly affected by stories within her family about her Hungarian relatives who were murdered during the Nazi Holocaust* during World War II.

A gifted scholar, she studied at Bennington College in Vermont before going on to Yale University. Butler had come out as a lesbian at 16 and at Yale she became active in lesbian and feminist politics.[4] She received her PhD in philosophy in 1984 for a study on the impact on French philosophy of the eighteenth-century German thinker Georg Wilhelm Friedrich Hegel.*

After graduating from Yale, she taught at several major American universities, including Wesleyan University and Johns Hopkins University, before being appointed Maxine Elliot Professor in Rhetoric and Comparative Literature at the University of California, Berkeley in 1990.[5] She is also Hannah Arendt Chair at the European Graduate School in Switzerland.

Her first book was a revised version of her doctoral thesis, *Subjects of Desire: Hegelian Reflections in Twentieth-Century France* (1987).[6] It was followed in 1990 by *Gender Trouble*, which catapulted her into the academic spotlight. Much of her work in the 1990s, starting with *Bodies That Matter: On the Discursive Limits of "Sex"* (1993),[7] was written to clarify the ideas set out in *Gender Trouble*. She has written or co-written more than a dozen books on gender, philosophy, and politics.[8] Butler has also become a high-profile and outspoken political commentator on the problems facing the world since the 9/11* terrorist attacks on America in 2001.

Author's Background

Butler's work explores two big themes—the oppression of minorities, and exclusion. These spring from her own experiences as a feminist Jewish lesbian. She says that Judaism* taught her it is "ethically imperative to speak up and to speak out" on prejudice, but also that she "grew very skeptical" of Jewish identity politics, and the forms of "separatism"* it fostered.[9] She did not like the way lesbians and feminists at Yale also set down rules dictating what qualified women to claim that identity, and decided that she could not "live in a world in which identity is being policed in this way."[10] The 1980s, when Butler was writing *Gender Trouble*, marked a turbulent period in struggles for women's rights and lesbian, gay, bisexual, and transsexual (LGBT)* rights. Identity issues were at the heart of these movements during this period.

After the huge gains made by the first wave of feminism in the United States, the Equal Rights Amendment* to the American Constitution, which would have guaranteed equal rights for women, stalled in 1979, and never made it into law. As the 1980s wore on, the second wave of feminism (dating from the 1960s) was fractured by infighting. Arguments raged around the status in the movement of trans* women (that is, people who do not identify with the sex assigned them at birth or by society at large), as well as around responses to pornography and often painful sexual activity involving bondage, domination, sadism and masochism (BDSM).* This led to polarized debates over censorship, what it meant to be a feminist, and even what it meant to be a woman.

At the same time, LGBT movements in the United States were struggling with their own inclusivity issues. Transgender and bisexual* individuals often felt marginalized for not being homosexual in the accepted sense.[11] These struggles all occurred against the backdrop of the AIDS* crisis, where the incurable syndrome that attacked the immune system decimated the gay community—and led to the stigma from society against gay men increasing.

This was the turbulent political and academic backdrop to the writing of *Gender Trouble*. Additionally, Butler also drew on personal issues much closer to home. Her family background included the oppression of minorities—her mother's aunts and uncles had all died in the Holocaust.*[12] She also had first-hand knowledge of the terrible damage inflicted by gender norms*—her uncle was "incarcerated for his anatomically anomalous body" and lived out his life in an institution on the Kansas prairies.[13] Butler describes *Gender Trouble* as springing from "a desire to live, to make life possible, and to rethink the possible."[14]

NOTES

1   Susan Bordo, "Postmodern Subjects, Postmodern Bodies," *Feminist Studies* 18, no. 1 (Spring 1992): 173.

2   Margaret Nash, "Review: *Gender Trouble: Feminism and the Subversion of Identity* by Judith Butler; *Homophobia: A Weapon of Sexism* by Suzanne Pharr," *Hypatia* 5, no. 3 (Autumn 1990): 171.

3   Bordo, "Postmodern Subjects," 174.

4   Judith Butler, "Interview," *Haaretz*, February 24, 2010, accessed June 5, 2015, http://www.haaretz.com/news/judith-butler-as-a-jew-i-was-taught-it-was-ethically-imperative-to-speak-up-1.266243.

5   Judith Butler, "Interview," *Lola Press Magazine*, May 2001, accessed June 5, 2015, http://www.lolapress.org/elec2/artenglish/butl_e.htm.

6   Judith Butler, *Subjects of Desire: Hegelian Reflections in Twentieth-Century France* (New York: Columbia University Press, 1987).

7   Judith Butler, *Bodies that Matter: On the Discursive Limits of "Sex"* (New York: Routledge, 1993).

8   Judith Butler, "Biography," accessed June 5, 2015, http://complit.berkeley.edu/?page_id=168.

9   Butler, "Interview," *Haaretz*.

10 Butler, "Interview," *Haaretz*.

11 Susan Stryker, "Transgender History, Homonormativity, and Disciplinarity," *Radical History Review* 2008, no. 100: 146.

12 Butler, "Interview," *Haaretz*.

13 Judith Butler, *Gender Trouble: Feminism and the Subversion of Identity* (Abingdon: Routledge, 1999).

14 Butler, *Gender Trouble*, xxi.

MODULE 2
ACADEMIC CONTEXT

KEY POINTS

- *Gender Trouble* is an interdisciplinary work—that is, it draws on the disciplines of philosophy, anthropology,* psychoanalysis,* and feminist theory* to investigate where our gender* identities come from.

- Ever since the work of the French thinker Simone de Beauvoir* in the 1940s, feminists* have explored the idea that genders are not natural* but formed by culture.

- Butler was greatly influenced by the poststructuralist* theorist Jacques Derrida* in questioning fundamental beliefs about sex and gender by studying the uncertainties of language and meaning (an approach typical of poststructuralist thought).

The Work In Its Context

In *Gender Trouble* Judith Butler draws on two areas of thought developed after World War II*—second-wave feminist philosophy, and "French theory."* Both have their roots in European philosophy from the nineteenth and twentieth centuries, and they share two key concerns.

The first is what philosophers call "subject formation"*—that is, the ways in which "personhood" is produced. The second is the relationship between culture, language, and power structures in society.

In the European (Continental philosophy)* tradition, "the subject" refers to the abstract idea of the individual person. So in this context, "subjectivity"* essentially means "personhood." This technical meaning is completely different from the everyday use of "subjectivity" to mean personal opinion. The term "subject formation" refers to the

> ❝ *Gender Trouble* is rooted in 'French Theory,' which is itself a curious American construction. Only in the United States are so many disparate theories joined together as if they formed some kind of unity. ❞
>
> Judith Butler, *Gender Trouble: Feminism and the Subversion of Identity*

way in which individual personhood is the result of natural, social, or cultural forces. Power structures in society (expressed in language, culture, and economic relationships) are an important factor in subject formation and central to Continental philosophy.

Gender Trouble focuses on late twentieth-century thinkers who share a common heritage in nineteenth-century Continental philosophy. Three key philosophers in this respect are the German philosopher Georg Wilhelm Friedrich Hegel,* the German economist and political philosopher Karl Marx,* and the German philosopher Friedrich Nietzsche.* Hegel's *Phenomenology of Spirit* (1807) traced the formation of human subjectivity through dialectics*—that is, ideas moving forward through the evolution of argument. Taking on Hegel's reasoning, Marx's *Capital* (1867) said that subjectivity is formed by people's economic conditions. Meanwhile, in texts such as *On the Genealogy of Morals* (1887), Nietzsche looked at fixed ideas of morality and how they have changed through history.

The influence of these earlier philosophers can be seen in Butler's work. Her first book, *Subjects of Desire*, investigates Hegel's reception in post-war French philosophy, and discusses Marx and Nietzsche at length. By reading the existentialist* philosophers Jean-Paul Sartre* and Simone de Beauvoir alongside later thinkers such as the psychoanalyst Jacques Lacan,* the historian and theorist Michel Foucault,* and the philosopher Jacques Derrida,* Butler joins the dots between the founders of Continental philosophy and the writers discussed in *Gender Trouble*.

Overview of the Field

In the post-war era* following World War II, European (Continental) feminists were focused on power relations between men and women, and on the difference between sex* (male/female) and gender* (masculine/feminine). In *The Second Sex* (1949), the French existentialist philosopher Simone de Beauvoir famously stated that "one is not born, but rather becomes, a woman."[1] So feminine behavior is not an inevitable consequence of female biology. Gender behavior is imposed on women by the norms of a male-dominated society.

Writers after de Beauvoir (second-wave feminists),* such as Catharine McKinnon* in America and Luce Irigaray* and Monique Wittig* in France, used this insight to investigate how patriarchy* (male-dominated culture and society) subordinated women through these norms. They also explored how femininity itself was part of the problem.

One example was feminine fashion over the ages. Women's clothes were often uncomfortable and impractical, limiting their mobility and therefore the activities they could take part in. By just trying to look good in the ways society values, women often reinforced the false idea that they were the "weaker sex." Second-wave feminism sought to uncover and challenge such processes.

France also saw the rise of what is known in American and British universities as "French theory." This refers to the thinkers whose works rose out of two movements: structuralism* (a theoretical approach to culture founded on the idea that culture comes from, and is given meaning by, larger "natural" structures understandable as oppositional pairs such as "raw" and "cooked"), and poststructuralism* (an approach which severs culture's connection with these hypothetical structures altogether, questioning the very possibility that we can arrive at an objective "truth" through analytical thought). Strongly influenced by Hegel and Marx, key figures in these schools of thought included the psychoanalyst Jacques Lacan, the feminist literary theorist Julia Kristeva,* the historian of power and sexuality Michel Foucault, and the philosopher Jacques Derrida. Butler brought their ways of working (especially those of Derrida) to bear on feminist histories of how personhood was formed.

Academic Influences

Butler is the first to admit that *Gender Trouble* has a very wide variety of influences and brings together "disparate theories" from writers "who had few alliances with each other."[2] That makes it difficult to neatly sum up the book's influences.[3] Butler was influenced, at one and the same time, by certain specific thinkers, by the complex tradition of Continental philosophy in general, and by the activist circles she moved in.

There are, however, five key figures in feminist thought and French theory whose direct influence is clear—and they are all quoted in the book's epigraph (the short quotation or quotations often used to open a book). These figures are de Beauvoir, Kristeva, Irigaray, Foucault, and Wittig.[4] Each of these writers is a source for a different aspect of Butler's approach to gender. From de Beauvoir comes the concern with becoming masculine or feminine. From Kristeva comes the close attention to language and semiotics* (the study of linguistic signs). From Irigaray comes the concern with psychoanalysis* (and in particular with the approach of Lacan). From Foucault comes the interest in social power structures while from Wittig, Butler takes the concern with gay and lesbian perspectives in feminism.[5]

Derrida is a great influence on Butler, being a founder of the poststructuralist approach she takes to culture and gender. Butler credits him with leading her thinking on "performativity"* (roughly, the idea that in *enacting*, for example, "femininity" or "masculinity," we actually *create* it in ourselves). Though in *Gender Trouble* she refers to him directly less frequently than any of the above writers, his influence runs through the whole book Derrida encourages the questioning of concepts often seen as unquestionable or fundamental—such as sex and gender—and the refusal to reach rigid conclusions.[6]

NOTES

1   Simone de Beauvoir, *The Second Sex*, trans. E. M. Pashley (New York: Vintage, 1973), 301.

2   Judith Butler, *Gender Trouble: Feminism and the Subversion of Identity* (Abingdon: Routledge, 1999).

3   See Gill Jagger, *Judith Butler: Sexual Politics, Social Change and the Power of the Performative* (Oxford: Routledge, 2008), 6.

4   Butler, *Gender Trouble*, i.

5   Butler, *Gender Trouble*, x–xi.

6   Butler, *Gender Trouble*, xv.

MODULE 3
THE PROBLEM

KEY POINTS

- During the 1980s, feminist,* lesbian, gay, bisexual,* and transsexual* movements were increasingly concerned with tensions over different identities.

- The appearance of subcategories such as "lesbian feminism," along with the recognition of prejudice within both feminism and gay and lesbian activism, made questions of gender identity extremely important.

- Butler intervened in these debates by questioning the very idea of stable gender identity.

Core Question

The questions at the heart of Judith Butler's *Gender Trouble* are: How do social expectations of gender and sexual identity result in the subjugation of minority groups? And how can rethinking identity help those groups?

These questions spring from developments in feminism from the 1960s onwards. Butler describes a shift in feminist theory from "[assuming] that there is some existing identity, understood through the category of women," to questioning if "woman" was a real category at all.[1] In other words, feminism involved the pursuit of equality for "women", which had been understood as an "essential" or natural* category that was not created by society. Butler's radical theory, however, brought "this prevailing conception" into question, highlighting that feminists actually had "very little agreement … on what it is that constitutes or ought to constitute the category of women."[2]

> ❝ It is not enough to inquire into how women might become more fully represented in language and politics. Feminist critique ought also to understand how the category of 'women,' the subject of feminism, is produced and restrained by the very structures of power through which emancipation is sought. ❞
>
> Judith Butler, *Gender Trouble: Feminism and the Subversion of Identity*

Butler's ambitious aim is to shift the question away from "What is a woman?" Instead, she asks two different questions: "How are gendered subjects*—that is, individuals—of any kind formed?" and "How does our culture limit the way different identities are represented?"

Representation is an important term here. The word has two senses; one signifies political representation (as in voting rights), and the other is the language we use to talk about gender identities, aside from just "masculine" and "feminine." For Butler, they are two halves of one fundamental question. Representing minorities politically means talking about them accurately. That is the key to understanding and communicating their humanity. "How," Butler asks, "must we rethink the ideal morphological* constraints upon the human such that those who fail to approximate the norm are not condemned to a death within life?"[3] By "morphological," she refers to the outward physical characteristics that commonly decide how we are perceived by others.

The Participants

Before *Gender Trouble*, many feminists based their struggle for equality on natural attributes and qualities that made women essentially different to men. This was an essentialist* approach, since it was built around the idea of an enduring "essence of woman" that pre-dated culture. Luce Irigaray followed this line in her controversial *This Sex Which Is Not One* (1976). She argued that real female identity is oppressed through a culture ruled by men. "We are women from the start," she wrote, "we don't have to be turned into women by [men]."[4]

By the time *Gender Trouble* appeared in 1990, these ideas had begun to be questioned. The French historian and cultural critic Michel Foucault* suggested that there were no such things as "essential identities." In other words, there could be no "women from the start." In his *History of Sexuality* (1976–1986) he suggests that identities such as "woman" (or "man," or "heterosexual"* and "homosexual"*) are not natural at all, but cultural. They are produced by what he calls *discourse*[*5]—roughly, a culture's values, beliefs, ideas, and practices.

The anthropologist Gayle Rubin's* influential essay "The Traffic in Women" (1975) followed a similar line of inquiry. She states that gender is not a natural identity but a "socially imposed" one.[6] For her, the very category of "woman" is part of society's domination of women: "We are not only oppressed as women," she wrote, "but by having to *be* women." These ideas paved the way for Butler, as Rubin's dream for liberation swapped an essentialist idea of "liberated woman" for a "genderless" society, "in which one's sexual anatomy is irrelevant to who one is."[7]

The Contemporary Debate

As Butler was writing *Gender Trouble* she knew that the academic world was shifting towards poststructuralism,* an approach to cultural analysis that challenged, among other things, notions of objective truth and the dependability of meaning itself. This was a radical departure from the traditions of earlier European philosophy (known as Continental philosophy),* and it dealt with two aspects of thought. These were hermeneutics* (that is, the philosophy of interpretation), and epistemology (the philosophy of knowledge—what we know and how we can know it).

For the philosopher Jacques Derrida,* a founder of poststructuralism, all knowledge exists in, and is produced by, language and culture. Knowledge is nothing beyond language. For something to be an object of knowledge, it must be understood as rooted in human culture, not in nature.[8] All knowledge, then, must be interpreted as a product of culture.

With scholars such as Rubin already making similar points, Derrida found favor among more radical feminists. Debates came down to whether "woman" was a natural or a cultural category. For those who followed in Derrida's footsteps, including the French lesbian theorist Monique Wittig,* the answer had to be that "woman," "gender," and "sex" were products of culture, not of nature.[9] Such a radical idea was controversial, however, as it questioned how feminism could even exist if "woman" was merely a cultural construct.

In the 1999 edition of *Gender Trouble*, Butler states that her work "turned out to be one of cultural translation," where "poststructuralist* theory was brought to bear on US theories of gender and the political predicaments of feminism."[10] She was very aware of the identity debates raging within feminism and sought to bring an outside perspective—that of poststructuralism—to the table.

NOTES

1 Judith Butler, *Gender Trouble: Feminism and the Subversion of Identity* (Abingdon: Routledge, 1999), 2.

2 Butler, *Gender Trouble*, 2.

3 Butler, *Gender Trouble*, xx.

4 Luce Irigaray, *This Sex Which is Not One*, trans. Catherine Porter (Ithaca, NY: Cornell University Press, 1985), 212.

5 Michel Foucault, *The History of Sexuality*, trans. Robert Hurley, 3 vols (Harmondsworth: Penguin, 1990).

6   Gayle Rubin, "The Traffic in Women: Notes on the 'Political Economy' of Sex," in *Toward an Anthropology of Women*, ed. Rayna Reiter (New York: Monthly Review Press, 1975), 204.

7   Rubin, "Traffic in Women," 204.

8   See Derrida's foundational 1966 lecture "Structure, Sign, and Play in the Discourse of the Human Sciences," in Jacques Derrida, *Writing and Difference*, trans. Alan Bass (Abingdon: Routledge, 2001).

9   See, for instance, Monique Wittig, "One is Not Born a Woman," in *The Straight Mind and Other Essays* (Boston: Beacon Press), 9–20.

10 Butler, *Gender Trouble*, ix.

MODULE 4
THE AUTHOR'S CONTRIBUTION

KEY POINTS

- Judith Butler argues that gender is brought into being by a person unconsciously acting in ways that are accepted to be "masculine" or "feminine"—and that even biological sex is a product of culture.

- Gender is imposed through patterns of thought woven into society, but history shows that identities have changed over time, so it is impossible to insist that they are fixed and eternal.

- *Gender Trouble* is an original and radical text that employs for political ends the analytical methods of poststructuralist* theory (and its challenge to categories and ideas of objective truth).

Author's Aims

Judith Butler begins *Gender Trouble* by noting the feminist fear of thinking too hard about the meaning of gender,* "as if the indeterminacy of gender might eventually culminate in the failure of feminism."[1] Butler does not share that fear. Her book tackles gender indeterminacy—that is, the problem of defining people by gender—head on in order to create new possibilities for liberation, both in and beyond feminism.

Butler argues that feminism's idea of "the category of women as a coherent and stable subject"* is an unwitting "reification* of gender relations."[2] By this, she means feminism's specific interest in women acts to "make real" the male–female opposition that is the basis of women's subjugation in society. That then reinforces society's

> 66 No political revolution is possible without a radical shift in one's notion of the possible and the real. 99
>
> Judith Butler, *Gender Trouble: Feminism and the Subversion of Identity*

"compulsory heterosexuality"* and heteronormativity* (the presumption that heterosexuality is "normal" and all other sexualities "abnormal"). This has the effect of limiting feminist solidarity with minorities.

The time has come, Butler suggests, "to ask what political possibilities are the consequence of a radical critique of the categories of identity."[3] What could happen to liberation movements for women or LGBT* individuals if we ask why and how people identify themselves as "women," or "gays," or "lesbians," or "trans"* in the first place? Instead of examining any one identity, Butler sets out to investigate the very basis of identity categories to explain how we develop and who ends up with power in society. "What new shape of politics," she asks, will emerge when feminism no longer sees feminine identity as its foundation, "when identity as a common ground no longer constrains the discourse on feminist politics?"[4]

Approach

Gender Trouble sets out to show that we are not born into a gender, but are shaped into one through our upbringing and the society we live in. Butler argues that "the foundational categories of sex, gender, and desire [homo/hetero/bisexuality]" are neither "real" nor "essential," but are instead "effects" of the way society is organized.[5] *Gender Trouble* "troubles" these identity categories by pointing out how they have changed throughout history. This proves they are not set in stone. If "female" or "gay" were fixed categories, they would come before culture and could not be changed by it; but if they can be shown to have changed across time, or to be different in different cultures, they cannot be certain.

Butler says that gender and sexuality are created by social "institutions, practices, [and] discourses"* (meaning the systems of language, belief, and action that belong to a culture at any given time); these things give gender and sexuality "the effect of the natural."*[6]

This process must not be seen as "deliberate," though. The "institutions" and "practices" she writes about are not conscious strategies to dominate women or minority sexualities. They are patterns of thought so deeply embedded in society that they are almost invisible. Butler's mission is to expose these patterns and offer a whole new way of understanding gender.

Two "institutions" play a crucial role in creating identity categories, according to *Gender Trouble*—"phallogocentrism"* and "compulsory heterosexuality."* The first refers to how Western culture is both "logocentric" (it assumes language gives the world real meaning) and "phallocentric" (it prefers the masculine over the feminine). Even language seen as neutral or objective, including scientific writing, is weighted toward a "male" worldview.

"Compulsory heterosexuality" describes how the widespread assumption that heterosexuality is natural (making other sexualities unnatural) acts to make people heterosexual. By examining these institutions, Butler shows that gender and sexuality categories are in no way natural and fixed, but produced through the pressures of society.

Contribution In Context

Gender Trouble's most original contribution is in applying poststructuralism to gender and sex. Although in their work the feminist thinkers Gayle Rubin* and Monique Wittig* both criticized the approach to cultural analysis known as structuralism,* no feminist theorist had used the theory to question the very idea of category itself.

As the work of the French philosopher Michel Foucault* shows, Butler was not the first to deconstruct sexuality and gender—but she took it much further. Foucault investigated sexuality's creation by "juridical* regimes,"*[7] (the law) and how power relations inscribe themselves on human bodies.[8] By this he is referring to a kind of labeling of the body that beds down into the body and the psyche.

Foucault did not, however, pursue his theory to what Butler saw as its natural end—namely, acceptance of the body itself as cultural. By making that leap, *Gender Trouble* marks a watershed moment in both feminism and philosophy more generally.

Before *Gender Trouble*, apart from Wittig in *One is Not Born a Woman*, thinkers worked on the assumption that the biological facts of a person's body, their sex, came before the impact of their culture. Butler, on the other hand, follows the logic of poststructuralism to the point of declaring that the body is "always already a cultural sign,"[9] suggesting that "perhaps this construct called 'sex' is as culturally constructed as gender."[10]

It is important to note *Gender Trouble*'s originality in turning poststructuralism towards political ends. Although Derrida had first talked of the poststructuralist "rupture" in 1966,[11] *Gender Trouble* marks the first point, outside of France, that this rupture was felt beyond the academic world.

NOTES

1   Judith Butler, *Gender Trouble: Feminism and the Subversion of Identity* (Abingdon: Routledge, 1999), xxix.

2   Butler, *Gender Trouble*, 7.

3   Butler, *Gender Trouble*, 7.

4   Butler, *Gender Trouble*, 7.

5   Butler, *Gender Trouble*, xxxi.

6   Butler, *Gender Trouble*, xxxi.

7   Michel Foucault, *The History of Sexuality*, trans. Robert Hurley, 3 vols (Harmondsworth: Penguin, 1990), vol. 1.

8   Michel Foucault, Discipline and Punish: The Birth of the Prison, trans. Alan Sheridan (Harmondsworth: Penguin, 1991).

9   Butler, Gender Trouble, 96.

10 Butler, Gender Trouble, 9–10.

11 Jacques Derrida, "Structure, Sign, and Play in the Discourse of the Human Sciences," in Jacques Derrida, Writing and Difference, trans. Alan Bass (Abingdon: Routledge, 2001).

SECTION 2
IDEAS

MODULE 5
MAIN IDEAS

KEY POINTS

- *Gender Trouble* tackles the "realness" of gender* and sexual identities, how social power structures are maintained through repeating gender performances, and the possibility for subverting the system by "troubling" our identities.

- Judith Butler says gender is performative,* which means that it is brought into being by the unconscious repetition of behavior accepted as masculine or feminine.

- Butler has been criticized for her difficult writing style but maintains that this is part of her argument for challenging how we use language to describe sex and gender.

Key Themes

Judith Butler's *Gender Trouble* argues that gender is not a "natural* fact," but a cultural construction. Although this is a view shared by other second-wave feminists* (feminists of the years following World War II,* notably in the 1960s), Butler takes it as a starting point to question the whole basis of feminism itself.

Butler's radical ideas explore the perception of women as a distinct group. As it is "impossible to separate 'gender' from the political and cultural intersections in which it is invariably produced and maintained,"[1] a movement that accepts "gender" as a foundation for its desires will reproduce the power relations of those intersections. An "intersection" here means a place where two forms of prejudice meet each other. White women might, for instance, be prejudiced against black women, or upper-class women might be prejudiced against lower-class women. And these intersections help maintain the lower place of women in society overall.

> ❝ Because there is neither an 'essence' that gender expresses or externalizes nor an objective ideal to which gender aspires, and because gender is not a fact, the various acts of gender create the idea of gender, and without those acts, there would be no gender at all. ❞
>
> Judith Butler, *Gender Trouble: Feminism and the Subversion of Identity*

Instead, Butler says, "a new sort of feminist politics is now desirable"—one that takes "the variable construction of identity as both a methodological and normative* prerequisite, if not a political goal."[2] In other words, by concentrating on those identified as "women," feminism reinforces the idea that men and women are different, and such an assumption is precisely what led to women's oppression in the first place. What is needed instead is a feminism that works by changing identities and promoting new forms of identity. Only then, according to Butler, can feminism escape the patterns of thought that lead to the subjugation of women.

Gender Trouble has four themes:

- Separating gender (roughly, the behaviors commonly used to distinguish "female" and "male") from sex (the biological attributes commonly used to distinguish "male" from "female") more fully than earlier feminists did, and exploring the consequences of this shift
- Understanding that the power of identity categories lies in the "reality effect" they are given by "discourse,"* instead of in "natural", "foundational,"* or "essential"* facts
- Viewing gender as a "performative" process of playing a role rather than as having a fixed status
- Exploring the potential to subvert gender norms in politics and wider culture.

Although these ideas are complex, *Gender Trouble*'s core idea can be summed up simply. Butler argues that because standard assumptions about identity have resulted in centuries of inequality, identity itself must be questioned and subverted.

Exploring the Ideas

If gender and sexuality are produced by culture—what Butler calls "social fictions"—how can they exercise such power over people? How is it that women and lesbian, gay, bisexual, and transsexual (LGBT*) people have been marginalized or subjugated by society?

The answer lies in "discourse." Discourse refers to all the cultural practices of society taken together. It includes all language, customs, and patterns of thought. As Foucault suggested, these are closely related to social organization and power structures, both of which are concepts that he devoted his career to analyzing, but that he approaches most famously in *Discipline and Punish* and volume 1 of *The History of Sexuality*.[3] For instance, using "straight" to mean "heterosexual"* reflects an assumption that heterosexuality is correct and normal and homosexuality* "bent," or incorrect and abnormal. This in turn implies that homosexuals are a minority, which also implies that they have less power than the "straight" majority. That this is still the case even in liberal societies shows how closely tied to language power structures can be.

Butler points out that discourse passes such assumptions on to every new generation—and power structures with them. We are all born into discourse so we cannot help but learn and repeat it. Gender is a key aspect of this. We learn how to "do gender right," just as we learn to speak English correctly. Like language, gender reflects and reproduces society's power structures. So gender is a "social fiction," but it is also powerfully real. Everywhere we look, we see gendered actions unconsciously repeated. When individuals perform their gender, their performances actually make gender exist.[4]

For these reasons, Butler defines gender as "performative". It is a performance that becomes real by being performed. This insight is the book's political center. If gender is something a person does, then a possibility opens up for doing it differently, subverting its performance to change social expectations. Butler draws the line at suggesting definite political action, though. Individuals have no choice but to repeat gendered actions and can only hope to do so in a way that "*displace*[s] the very gender norms that enable the repetition itself."[5] Exactly what such a displacement would mean, however, Butler does not say.

Language and Expression

Gender Trouble is a challenging book and Butler has often been criticized for her writing style. In 1998 she won *Philosophy and Literature*'s "Bad Writing Contest" for what the journal's editor, Dennis Dutton, called the "anxiety-inducing obscurity" of her writing.[6] She also received deeper critiques from the philosopher Martha Nussbaum, who accused her of using "obscurantist sleight-of-hand" to avoid openly debating her ideas.[7]

Part of *Gender Trouble*'s difficulty lies in its reliance on the technical vocabulary of Continental* (European) philosophy of the nineteenth and twentieth centuries. Understanding the key terms Butler uses goes a long way towards solving this problem. It is also true, however, that Butler deliberately employs a "complicated and challenging" style, "in the service of calling taken-for-granted truths into question."[8] This complicated style is related to the arguments of *Gender Trouble* itself. For Butler, "neither grammar nor style are politically neutral," and troubling the norms of grammar is one way of challenging political norms.[9] One example of this is the attempt to shift "gender" from a noun to a verb. As Butler writes, "If gender itself is naturalized through grammatical norms ... then the alteration of gender at the most fundamental epistemic level will be conducted, in part, through contesting the grammar in which gender is given."[10] Within standard grammar, "gender," a noun, is fixed. But in Butler's new grammar, "gender" becomes a verb, so it no longer needs to be fixed, opening up possibilities for subversion and play.[11]

NOTES

1   Judith Butler, *Gender Trouble: Feminism and the Subversion of Identity* (Abingdon: Routledge, 1999), 4–5.

2   Butler, *Gender Trouble*, 7–8.

3   Michel Foucault, *Discipline and Punish: The Birth of the Prison*, trans. Alan Sheridan (Harmondsworth: Penguin, 1991); Michel Foucault, *The History of Sexuality*, trans. Robert Hurley, 3 vols (Harmondsworth: Penguin, 1990), vol. 1.

4   The history of the term "performativity" is brief but complex, but for a brief summary and explanation of its origins in J. L. Austin's work on "speech acts" see Oliver Belas, "Performativity," in *The Encyclopedia of Literary and Cultural Theory*, ed. Gregory Castle, Robert Eaglestone, and M. Keith Booker (Oxford: Blackwell Publishing, 2011), 519.

5   Butler, *Gender Trouble*, 203.

6   Dennis Dutton, "The Bad Writing Contest: Press Releases, 1996–1998," accessed June 5, 2015, http://denisdutton.com/bad_writing.htm.

7   Martha C. Nussbaum, "The Professor of Parody", in *Philosophical Interventions: Reviews, 1986–2011* (Oxford: Oxford University Press, 2012), 203.

8   Butler, *Gender Trouble*, xix.

9   Butler, *Gender Trouble*, xix.

10 Butler, *Gender Trouble*, xx.

11 Butler, *Gender Trouble*, 34.

MODULE 6
SECONDARY IDEAS

KEY POINTS

- Judith Butler says some statements about identity (and crucially, "women") ignore how different identities overlap and suffer prejudice, and she also points to literature as a way to trouble the language for sex and gender.

- Butler is not credited as one of its originators, but this idea of overlapping identities — called intersectionality* — is now a central topic in feminist* and lesbian, gay, bisexual, and transsexual theory.

- The implications of *Gender Trouble* for literary studies have been huge, with gender* identity now a central topic for many scholars.

Other Ideas

One of Judith Butler's secondary ideas in *Gender Trouble* is that different categories of identity can interact in ways that subjugate and marginalize certain people.

A universal idea of "women" that assumes they all belong to a single coherent category runs the risk of leaving the "dimensions of class and racial privilege intact."[1] By this, she means that we must pay attention to the ways, for instance, African Americans or lesbians experience their female identity differently to straight, white women and suffer from other forms of prejudice such as racism or homophobia.* These forms of prejudice can "intersect" with one another to keep specific groups on the margins of society. This is known as "intersectionality," and while *Gender Trouble* deals with it only briefly, it is important to the book's overall argument.

> **❝** The literary text as war machine is ... directed against the hierarchical division of gender, the splitting of universal and particular in the name of a recovery of a prior and essential unity of those terms. **❞**
>
> Judith Butler, *Gender Trouble: Feminism and the Subversion of Identity*

Another secondary idea has actually come to define *Gender Trouble*'s impact on literary theory. It is that literature might be particularly useful in exploring gender, sex, and sexuality. It is no accident that several of the feminist theorists discussed in *Gender Trouble* (including de Beauvoir, Wittig and Kristeva) also had distinguished careers as novelists, using fiction to explore their philosophy. Butler's own philosophical approach, working through close attention to language, has strong ties with literary criticism and points the way for critics who discuss gender in books.

Exploring the Ideas

There is no question that intersectionality has been a dominant trend in feminist theory since the beginning of the twenty-first century.[2] The critical theorist Kimberlé Crenshaw* introduced the term as an *-ality* in 1989, the year before *Gender Trouble* was published.[3] Though Butler does not refer to intersection*ality* in the book, her discussion of "intersections" between forms of prejudice secures a place for *Gender Trouble* at the start of this major trend in contemporary feminism.

Butler deals quite quickly with the idea of intersecting prejudices before moving on to her main project of exposing identity categories themselves as social fictions. So "intersectionality" is present in Butler's poststructuralist* account of gender, but she aims to give a more ambitious explanation to demystify identity. The gender studies scholar Kathy Davis says that this is important to understanding the prominence of intersectionality[4] that followed *Gender Trouble*. Butler's radically open-ended analyses of identity helped the less radical but still progressive concept of intersectionality get a foothold in academic circles.

The literary nature of Butler's writing is fundamental to her ideas. Although *Gender Trouble* is not a work of literary analysis, she makes her case using the same technique—a detailed examination of a text, which is known as close-reading* (in which, for works for literature, authorial intention is irrelevant). She is very aware of the complex relationship between discourse* and literature, and her philosophy is a means of reading the world.

This relationship with literature can be seen throughout *Gender Trouble*. Butler says that the philosopher Derrida's* analysis of the Czech writer Franz Kafka's* short story *Before the Law* gave her her first insight into performativity.* She returns to Kafka when discussing "cultural inscription" on the human body.[5] In a different vein, her disagreement with Foucault's reading of the journals of the nineteenth-century hermaphrodite (that is, intersex individual) Herculine Barbin comes out of understanding the literary conventions of the classics and French romanticism.[6] Butler does not elaborate on Wittig's* description of books as a "war machine" against inequality. However, *Gender Trouble* also argues that literature offers liberating possibilities in gender performativity.

Overlooked

Gender Trouble is such a well-read landmark text in the fields of gender studies, feminism, and literary theory that it is difficult to claim it has any "overlooked" ideas. That said, one core aspect that is occasionally underplayed is Butler's suggestion that the either/or division of sexual morphology* (external biology) into male and female is itself a creation of discourse.

As she puts it, "sex proves to have been gender from the start"—a cultural fiction.[7] There is actually a wide spectrum of sexual characteristics between "male" and "female" in humans but discourse has reduced that spectrum to an either/or choice. A person must be male or female. According to Butler, the idea that it is "natural"* to be purely one or the other is as much a cultural fiction as masculine/ feminine gender characteristics.

This radical idea has been roundly criticized, especially by the feminist philosopher Martha Nussbaum.* Public debates on transgender and transsexual* rights, though, and the increasing acceptance of transgender people in public life may prove it is an idea whose time has come. The social scientist Gill Jagger* suggests that *Gender Trouble* opens up the whole conversation about seeing people only as male or female: "trans* experiences could contribute … to what Butler describes as the 'remapping of sexual difference' and could thus contribute towards rearticulating the [dominant] symbolic in a non-binary* form" (that is, they could help in accounting for the fact that the duality of "female/male" is not perfectly adequate as a means to understand sexual difference). [8]

NOTES

1   Judith Butler, *Gender Trouble: Feminism and the Subversion of Identity* (Abingdon: Routledge, 1999), 19.

?   Maria Carbin and Sara Edenheim, "The Intersectional Turn in Feminist Theory: A Dream of a Common Language? *European Journal of Woman's Studies* 20, no. 3 (August 2013).

3   Kimberlé Crenshaw, "Demarginalizing the Intersection of Race and Sex: A Black Feminist Critique of Antidiscrimination Doctrine, Feminist Theory and Antiracist Politics," *University of Chicago Legal Forum*, 1989.

4   See Kathy Davis "Intersectionality as Buzzword: A Sociology of Science Perspective on What Makes a Feminist Theory Successful," *Feminist Theory* 9, no. 1 (April 2008), 78–9.

5   Butler, *Gender Trouble*, xv, 177.

6   Butler, *Gender Trouble*, 134.

7   Butler, *Gender Trouble*, 154.

8   Gill Jagger, *Judith Butler: Sexual Politics, Social Change and the Power of the Performative* (Abingdon: Routledge, 2008), 157.

MODULE 7
ACHIEVEMENT

KEY POINTS

- The success of *Gender Trouble* can be seen in the rise of queer theory.*

- The book channeled a number of trends in feminist* and lesbian, gay, bisexual, and transsexual theory, making it a key text for those communities.

- Although Judith Butler is among today's most famous feminist thinkers, her writing is dauntingly difficult to grasp and as a result often misunderstood, misrepresented, or simply rejected.

Assessing The Argument

Judith Butler's central argument in *Gender Trouble: Feminism and the Subversion of Identity* is that identity categories are created by society and can be subverted. The scholars Warren Blumenfeld and Margaret Sönser Breen of the *International Journal of Sexuality and Gender Studies* have noted that these ideas "affected (and effectively shaped) many different fields of inquiry, including gender and sexuality studies, feminist and queer theory, and cultural studies."[1] Butler did not realize this would happen, saying that "the life of the text has exceeded my intentions."[2]

This can be seen as signaling *Gender Trouble*'s success in the emerging field of queer theory, a field which does not commonly present cut-and-dried conclusions but attempts to "trouble" its readers' assumptions in thought-provoking ways. Instead of providing fixed answers about identity, Butler deliberately takes the "rare" step of "closing on questions left in suspense."[3] By destabilizing widely

> ❝ [In] the decade since the publication of *Gender Trouble* ... few, if any, feminist theorists have been as influential or as controversial as Judith Butler. ❞
>
> Edwina Barvosa-Carter, *Butler Matters*

accepted positions on identity, turning assumptions into questions, Butler achieved precisely what she set out to do.

That said, Butler spent much of the early 1990s clarifying, revising, and reconsidering her views on: the human body (in *Bodies that Matter*, 1993); the category of "women" (in *Feminists Theorize the Political*, also 1993); and performativity* (throughout *Bodies that Matter* and publications that followed). This was necessary, as Butler noted, partly because of the confusions caused by the difficulty of *Gender Trouble*.[4] Also, her views changed as she became more politically active and chaired the International Gay and Lesbian Human Rights Commission (IGLHRC)* from 1994 to 1997.[5]

Achievement in Context

Gender Trouble sold more than 100,000 copies on its first publication and was read both inside and outside academic circles throughout the English-speaking world.[6] Its success was bolstered in North America and Britain by being widely reviewed in both academic and non-academic publications (most notably the New York gay weekly *Outweek*). It also had high-profile academic fans such as the literary theorist Gayatri Chakravorty Spivak,* who helped it onto the syllabus across the United States.[7] Circulation was also boosted by the strength of feminist academic networks in the United States, mainly around progressive universities on the East Coast, and the prestigious women's colleges known as the Seven Sisters.* A student at one, Barnard College, even produced two issues of a fanzine* called *Judy!*[8]

One of the notable achievements of *Gender Trouble* has been its reception outside of academia. Butler's work was important in the rise of lesbian, gay, bisexual, and transsexual (LGBT)* organizations and the international Pride movement* throughout the 1990s. *Gender Trouble* was quickly taken up by groups such as Queer Nation and Act Up at the center of US LGBT activism in the wake of the AIDS* crisis.[9] Even more strikingly, Butler's work was used as evidence in a major 1990s shake up of medical guidelines on homosexuality by the American Psychoanalytic Association and the American Psychological Association.[10]

Limitations

Despite the success of *Gender Trouble*, there have been hurdles to Butler reaching a wider readership. Of these, the principal problem is simply how difficult the book is to read and understand. Even in the English-speaking world, *Gender Trouble* remains an intimidating text. Misreadings of the book prompted Butler to return to some of its central concepts in *Bodies that Matter*. She realized, though, that "as an attempt to clarify my 'intentions,' [*Bodies that Matter*] appears destined to produce a new set of misapprehensions."[11]

Also, a lack of translations into other languages was a problem in the 1990s.[12] Although it is currently available in 13 languages other than English (including Turkish and Chinese), before the year 2000 the only translation available was in German.[13] Even though *Gender Trouble* is so dependent on French thought, no French translation appeared until 2005.

Butler's work on identity politics* (that is, political arguments focusing on the interests of particular groups marked out as having an exclusive identity) has expanded beyond gender and sexuality to take in ethnic identities. In these matters people are less willing to accept her poststructuralist* method of questioning fundamental beliefs about who we really are. Her contributions to debates on the Israel–Palestine conflict have resulted in accusations of anti-Semitism,* with her attempts to decenter identity politics proving extremely controversial in both Israel and international Jewish communities.[14] Butler's idea that fixed identities cause social problems—particularly between different communities in Israel—has been taken as an attack on Judaism,* despite her being Jewish herself.

NOTES

1   Warren J. Blumenfeld and Margaret Sönser Breen, "Introduction," *International Journal of Sexuality and Gender Studies*, Special Issue: Butler Matters: Judith Butler's Impact on Feminist and Queer Studies since *Gender Trouble* 6, nos. 1–2 (April 2001): 1.

2   Judith Butler, *Gender Trouble: Feminism and the Subversion of Identity* (Abingdon: Routledge, 1999), i.

3   Pierre Mayol, "Compte rendu: Judith Butler, *Trouble dans le genre: pour un feminisme de la subversion*," Agora 41, no. 41 (2006): 142.

4   Judith Butler, *Bodies that Matter: On the Discursive Limits of "Sex"* (New York: Routledge, 1993), 23.

5   Butler, *Gender Trouble*, xviii.

6   See Elena Loizidou, *Judith Butler: Ethics, Law, Politics* (Abingdon: Routledge, 2014), 1.

7   Susan Bordo, "Postmodern Subjects, Postmodern Bodies," *Feminist Studies* 18, no. 1 (Spring 1992): 174.

8   Available from "The Queer Zine Archive", accessed June 5, 2015, http://www.qzap.org/v5/gallery/main.php.

9   Butler, *Gender Trouble*, xviii.

10 Butler, *Gender Trouble*, xviii.

11 Butler, *Bodies that Matter*, xii.

12 See e.g. Lisa Downing and Robert Gillett (eds.), *Queer in Europe: Contemporary Case Studies* (Farnham: Ashgate, 2011), 115.

13 Figures taken from https://www.worldcat.org/, accessed June 5, 2015.

14 See e.g. Benjamin Weinthal, "Envoy to Germany: Awardee Ignores Terror on Israel," *Jewish Post*, August 28, 2012, accessed June 5, 2015, http://www.jpost.com/Jewish-World/Jewish-News/Envoy-to-Germany-Awardee-ignores-terror-on-Israel.

MODULE 8
PLACE IN THE AUTHOR'S LIFE AND WORK

KEY POINTS

- Judith Butler's work has become increasingly political since 2001, but her main concerns are still subjectivity (or personhood), and how groups and individuals deal with questions of identity.

- *Gender Trouble* was Butler's first widely read book, and remained the cornerstone of her work until she turned to other topics in the wake of the 9/11* terrorist attacks on America in 2001.

- *Gender Trouble* remains far and away the best known and most studied of Butler's books.

Positioning

Judith Butler was not a famous academic when *Gender Trouble* was published in 1990. Her first book, *Subjects of Desire* (1987), explores the impact and influence of the work of the philosopher Hegel* in France. Despite its title, it does not examine sex, sexuality, or gender. It features philosophers who later become important to Butler (the psychoanalyst Lacan* and the theorists Foucault* and Derrida*), but it does not have the same themes as *Gender Trouble*.

Gender Trouble was a significant departure from her earlier work. Written to expand on two articles she wrote for academic journals in 1986 and 1988, the book has defined her career.[1] The biggest change was the turn towards poststructuralism,* which has remained a key feature of her writing and political commentary.

> ❝ In this text as elsewhere I have tried to understand what political agency might be, given that it cannot be isolated from the dynamics of power from which it is wrought ... In some ways, the continuing work of that clarification, in response to numerous excellent criticisms, guides most of my subsequent publications. ❞
>
> Judith Butler, *Gender Trouble: Feminism and the Subversion of Identity*

Butler's 1990s output made use of poststructural methods in *Bodies that Matter: On the Discursive Limits of "Sex"* (1993), *Excitable Speech: A Politics of the Performative* (1997), and *The Psychic Life of Power: Theories in Subjection* (1997). These books are dedicated to explaining *Gender Trouble's* central ideas about performativity* and about the relationship between the body and identity and between language and subjectivity* (or personhood). She wrote them for people who misunderstood her the first time around, or because she had refined her thinking.

Bodies that Matter puts the readers right who saw her "performative" concept of gender as meaning people are completely free to choose their gender. Not so, says Butler, because any choice is severely limited by what society expects. *Excitable Speech* spells out more precisely what it means for language to be performative, highlighting how it can make or damage individuals. *The Psychic Life of Power*, meanwhile, goes into greater depth on the relationship between people's identity and how power in society is developed and maintained.

Butler's 1990s books bring new angles to the central themes of *Gender Trouble*, but don't change the basic theories. Each text returns to the question of "political agency."* Butler continues to ask what power individuals have to act in the world to change society for the better.

Integration

Though her focus has shifted away from gender since the start of the new millennium, Butler's work still forms a coherent whole. Everything she writes reveals a fascination with what we believe it takes to be human. Her recent books on kinship* explore this through looking at the ways people see themselves as related to others.

In *Antigone's Claim: Kinship Between Life and Death* (2000),[2] *Precarious Life: Powers of Mourning and Violence* (2004),[3] and *Frames of War: When is Life Grievable?* (2009),[4] Butler presents kinship as "the precondition of the human."[5] To be human we have to be recognized by other humans as "related" to them. We also need to recognize others as related to us. In the same way that gender and sexuality do, kinship makes other people real for us. It allows (or forces) us to treat them as humans who deserve equal rights.

Recently Butler has turned to studying how we mourn the dead—and who qualifies for our grief. Her arguments show a line of thought that reaches all the way from *Gender Trouble* through to her controversial contribution to the Israel–Palestine* debate, *Parting Ways: Jewishness and the Critique of Zionism* (2012). For Butler, to be a "grievable" subject* (roughly, a person whose loss can be grieved), you have to belong (to be "kin"), and be recognized as sharing an identity with the people doing the grieving. Although mourning is not explicitly discussed in *Gender Trouble*, Butler has called "grievability" the thread that "has linked my work on queer politics … with my more contemporary work on Israel-Palestine."[6]

Significance

Gender Trouble is Butler's most famous book and has had the greatest reach across academic disciplines and in the public debate. According to the second edition of the *Norton Anthology of Theory and Criticism*, *Gender Trouble* was "the most influential theoretical text of the 1990s."[7]

Feminist author and professor Lynne Huffer* says the book established Butler as one of the "three feminist founding thinkers of queer theory"* along with Gayle Rubin* and Eve Kosofsky Sedgwick.*[8] By "distill[ing] forty years of French theory,"* Butler has perhaps done more than anyone else to bring clarity and definition to the body of thinkers associated with the curious interdisciplinary assemblage known simply as "theory."[9]

Although Butler is a prolific writer, *Gender Trouble* still defines her reputation despite her output in the past quarter century. Thanks to her, "*gender trouble*" and "performativity" are now central concepts in literary criticism. Moreover, though she did not invent the word "performativity," her exploration of the concept is widely seen as being the most influential modern use of it.[10] Butler's later work often returns to the key ideas in *Gender Trouble*, ensuring that it remains the cornerstone of her reputation.

NOTES

1   Judith Butler, "Sex and Gender in Simone de Beauvoir's Second Sex," *Yale French Studies* 72 (1986); Judith Butler, "Performative Acts and Gender Constitution: An Essay in Phenomenology and Feminist Theory," *Theatre Journal* 40, no. 4 (December 1988).

2   Judith Butler, *Antigone's Claim: Kinship between Life and Death* (New York: Columbia University Press, 2000).

3   Judith Butler, *Precarious Life: The Powers of Mourning and Violence* (London: Verso, 2004).

4   Judith Butler, *Frames of War: When is Life Grievable?* (London: Verso, 2009).

5   Butler, *Antigone's Claim*, 82.

6   Judith Butler, "Interview," Haaretz, February 24, 2010, accessed June 5, 2015, http://www.haaretz.com/news/judith-butler-as-a-jew-i-was-taught-it-was-ethically-imperative-to-speak-up-1.266243

7   Vincent B. Leitch, et al. (eds.), *The Norton Anthology of Theory and Criticism* (New York and London: W. W. Norton and Company, 2001), 2536.

8   Lynne Huffer, *Mad for Foucault: Rethinking the Foundations of Queer Theory* (New York: Columbia University Press, 2010), 91.

9   Leitch et al., *Norton Anthology of Theory*, 2536.

10 Oliver Belas, "Performativity," in *The Encyclopedia of Literary and Cultural Theory*, ed. Gregory Castle, Robert Eaglestone, and M. Keith Booker (Oxford: Blackwell Publishing, 2011), 519.

SECTION 3
IMPACT

MODULE 9
THE FIRST RESPONSES

KEY POINTS

- Criticisms of *Gender Trouble* tend to run along two lines—namely, the difficulty of Butler's writing style, and the question of whether her ideas can make any actual difference in the real world.

- Judith Butler accused her critics of confusing postmodernism* (a challenge to society's deepest beliefs) with nihilism* (a belief in nothing).

- The reception of *Gender Trouble* was tied up with a widespread dislike of poststructuralist* writing generally, and Butler was caught in the crossfire of the Theory Wars* of the 1980s and 1990s—a time of fierce academic debate about the validity and usefulness of the strand of contemporary thought known as "theory".

Criticism

Gender Trouble: Feminism and the Subversion of Identity has attracted a good deal of criticism. This ranges from positions that remain broadly favorable towards Judith Butler, to those that accuse her of undermining the very foundations of feminism.

The most famous response to Butler is philosopher Martha Nussbaum's scathing 1999 review of *Gender Trouble, Bodies that Matter, Excitable Speech,* and *The Psychic Life of Power.* Labeling Butler "the Professor of Parody," Nussbaum accuses her of using "obscurantist sleight-of-hand" to avoid trading "arguments and counterarguments" with other philosophers.[1] More damningly, Nussbaum argues that Butler's position is one of "hip quietism"* (an acceptance of the way things are, and a refusal to resist or to attempt to change them). In suggesting that people can only subvert social norms through repeating

> **❝**It is hard to think of a writer whose work has been more prominently upheld as an example of bad academic writing than the philosopher and literary theorist Judith Butler. **❞**
>
> Cathy Birkenstein, "We Got the Wrong Gal"

them, Butler, Nussbaum claims, neglects social change so fully that she "collaborates with evil."[2]

Nussbaum's criticism is extreme but shows the strength of feminist objections to Butler's work, and to postmodern/poststructuralist feminism in general. Butler is seen as trading real social change for what can at best be called, in her own words, "an ironic hopefulness."[3] A more sympathetic critic is the Turkish American philosopher Seyla Benhabib.* She says: "Postmodernism can teach us the theoretical and political traps of why utopias* [perfect societies] … can go wrong, but it should not lead to a retreat from utopia altogether. For we, as women, have much to lose by giving up the utopian hope."[4] Women should not give up the hope of a perfect world brought about by political change, even if Butler's work on identity teaches us to be wary of such ideas.

Responses

Butler has not engaged directly with the more extreme critics of *Gender Trouble*, but did respond to Benhabib at the Greater Philadelphia Philosophy Consortium in 1990. Butler defends her position by questioning the use of the term "postmodern." Her critics, she argues, use it as shorthand for "nihilism," the belief in nothing at all. However, questioning concepts people take for granted, such as gender, she claims, is not the same as believing in nothing.[5] Such ideas should be questioned because this is precisely what triggers political change. Any movement committed to democratic change "needs to find a way to bring into question the foundations it is compelled to lay down."[6] For real change to occur without unconsciously repeating old political patterns, we have to question our most basic assumptions.

At the same time, Butler notes, "there are no *necessary* political consequences for such a theory … only a *possible* political deployment."[7] Her growing involvement in politics during the 1990s, and in the aftermath of the 9/11* attacks of 2001, shows that she does act on such possibilities. Engaging in world affairs should be recognized as Butler's practical answer to her critics. This includes her time chairing the International Gay and Lesbian Human Rights Commission (IGLHRC) in the 1990s, and her contributions to the Israel–Palestine debate* after 2001.

Conflict and Consensus

Criticism of *Gender Trouble* should be seen in light of the broader debate over "theory" (complex writing that questions standard academic and social assumptions) that reached its height in the "Theory Wars"* of the 1980s and 1990s. This consisted of heated academic rows over how useful theory was in the humanities. As the queer theorist Lisa Duggan pointed out, Butler was a primary target for any critic who saw theory as "jargonistic elitist obscurantism."[8] The Bad Writing Award that targeted Butler (along with other theorists) was a product of such thinking and still affects her reception today.

The height of the Theory Wars came in 1996, when physicist Alan Sokal succeeded in having a hoax postmodernist article published in the reputable journal *Social Text*. Titled *Transgressing the Boundaries: Toward a Transformative Hermeneutics of Quantum Gravity*, the piece lampooned theory by applying the work of Lacan,* Irigaray,* and Derrida* to physics. When the paper appeared, Sokal revealed the hoax and used it to criticize postmodernism. His main target was social constructivism* (theories, such as Butler's, that treat key ideas as having no existence outside of human culture and discourse). This, in

Sokal's view, could have no relevance to physics or most other areas of scientific inquiry.

Though Butler was not mentioned in the hoax, Sokal then wrote *Fashionable Nonsense*, a book that takes aim at the writers she uses in her work—Derrida, Lacan, Kristeva,* and Irigaray.[9] Duggan notes that Sokal's general critique was quickly developed into pointed attacks on postmodern feminism* and Butler herself.[10]

Now the Theory Wars have died down, *Gender Trouble* seems less controversial. Though consensus can hardly be said to exist, Butler's method has proved its usefulness across the field of literary criticism, where postmodernism is less likely to provoke disbelief or anger than it is in areas of scientific inquiry.

NOTES

1   Martha C. Nussbaum, "The Professor of Parody", in *Philosophical Interventions: Reviews, 1986–2011* (Oxford: Oxford University Press, 2012), 203.

2   Nussbaum, "The Professor of Parody," 215.

3   Judith Butler, *Excitable Speech: A Politics of the Performative* (New York and London: Routledge, 1997), 100.

4   Seyla Benhabib, "Feminism and Postmodernism: An Uneasy Alliance," in *Feminist Contentions: A Philosophical Exchange*, ed. Seyla Benhabib (New York: Routledge, 1995), 30.

5   See Judith Butler, "Contingent Foundations: Feminism and the Question of 'Postmodernism'," in *Feminist Contentions: A Philosophical Exchange*, ed. Seyla Benhabib (New York: Routledge, 1995), 30.

6   Butler, "Contingent Foundations," 41.

7   Butler, "Contingent Foundations," 41 (my emphasis).

8   Lisa Duggan, "The Theory Wars, or, Who's Afraid of Judith Butler?" *Journal of Women's History* 10, no. 1 (Spring 1998), 10.

9   See Alan Sokal and Jean Bricmont, *Fashionable Nonsense: Postmodern Intellectuals' Abuse of Science* (New York: Picador, 1998) (the book also contains the full text of the parody).

10 Duggan, "The Theory Wars," 12.

MODULE 10
THE EVOLVING DEBATE

KEY POINTS

- *Gender Trouble*'s arguments for taking a radical new look at gender identity helped to transform both political and literary responses to the topic.

- Most notably, *Gender Trouble* is considered a founding text of queer theory.*

- Butler has had a profound effect on every area of critical theory, with her vocabulary and ideas in widespread use among a variety of modern scholars.

Uses And Problems

Gender Trouble: Feminism and the Subversion of Identity by Judith Butler has deeply affected how people think about identity. This has been felt throughout the academic world (in the fields of philosophy, literature, and politics) and beyond into feminist* and lesbian, gay, bisexual, and transsexual (LGBT*) politics.

The social scientist Gill Jagger* describes this as "a shift from identity politics* based on sameness and the policing of boundaries" to one involving "the continual examination of the (political) construction of identities, and careful attention to the exclusions on which any identities are based."[1] The philosopher Slavoj Žižek* called this shift the "anti-identitarian turn of queer politics" that led to a fundamental change in feminist and LGBT thought.[2] The LGBT community has been shaped by many factors. However, the period after *Gender Trouble*'s publication saw gay activism become a broader movement for those who did not fit the label "heterosexual."*[3]

> **❝** Is theory still 'poststructuralism' or has that very term become meaningless precisely as its dissemination and contamination in cultural and political analysis establishes a set of unanticipated meanings for the term? In a sense, the value of poststructuralism no longer forms the pivot of contemporary debate, but, rather, its place in new forms of cultural and political analysis is both inchoate and central. **❞**
>
> Judith Butler, John Guillory and Kendall Thomas, *What's Left of Theory?*

For scholars, 1990 was a watershed year in literary theory—especially queer theory. Along with *Gender Trouble*, it was the year Eve Kosofsky Sedgwick's* *Epistemology of the Closet* and David Halperin's* *One Hundred Years of Homosexuality* were published. These texts share themes and concerns with *Gender Trouble* and helped to spread concepts such as social constructivism* (the idea that reality is a product of culture) and performativity* among writers, researchers, and thinkers.[4]

Schools of Thought

The key school of thought influenced by Butler's work is queer theory, the field that challenges what society deems "normal." However, it is only in retrospect that *Gender Trouble* has been recognized as a founding work. As the queer theorist David Halperin notes, Butler's theory was one whose time had come.[5]

Though the growth and acceptance of queer theory has been accompanied by changes in its nature, it always concentrates on "postmodern* identity." Queer theory is hard to pin down. It examines the analytical possibilities that come with destabilizing identity so it is continuously in flux. That's why critics as diverse as Michael Warner* and Jack/Judith Halberstam* have been identified as queer theorists, even though it is hard to see their work on topics as diverse as the "public sphere"*[6] and the singer Lady Gaga[7] as part of the same movement or as belonging to a single methodology.

This is the key to *Gender Trouble*'s relevance. As Halperin writes, "Queer is by definition whatever is at odds with the normal, the legitimate, the dominant. There is nothing in particular to which it necessarily refers. It is an identity without an essence."[8] It is, as professor of English Sara Salih notes, centered around looking at cultural documents (books, films, and art) in order to diagnose and "affirm the instability and indeterminacy of *all* gendered and sexed identities." In other words, in order to find—and cause—*gender trouble.*

In Current Scholarship

The language and ideas in *Gender Trouble*, especially concerning gender performativity, have spread through all areas of critical theory. As a result they have prompted "queering" inquiries in a number of fields. In literary studies, Butler's work has been used in criticism on sexuality and performance in the medieval* and Early Modern* periods. The first decade and a half of the twenty-first century has seen a steady flow of monographs and collections that investigate gender and sexuality using the tools of Butler's work and later queer theory.

Medievalist Glenn Burger* uses Butler alongside leading queer theorists Eve Kosofsky Sedgwick* and Lee Edelman* to understand Geoffrey Chaucer's reimagining of "medieval relations between the body and the community."[9] For Burger, performativity allows us to understand the pilgrim speakers of Chaucer's *The Canterbury Tales* as "subjects-in-process,""citing" the different types of identities expected in medieval times. Burger is not alone in a field that has embraced the implications of *Gender Trouble*. Fellow medievalist Bill Burgwinkle* noted: "The political and contingent are far more essential to an understanding of medieval texts than are the universal and essentializing* categories of men or women, homo or hetero."[10]

Early modernists studying the sixteenth, seventeenth, and eighteenth centuries have welcomed discoveries made by reading through Butler's eyes. Studies such as Carla Freccero's* important *Queer/Early/Modern* (2006) adopt Butler's method, as do countless other books and articles on early modern theater. Madhavi Menon, editor of *Shakesqueer: A Queer Companion to the Complete Works of Shakespeare* (2011), says it is no surprise that an art form defined by all-male performance and self-conscious performativity is fertile ground for Butler's theories.[11]

NOTES

1   Gill Jagger, *Judith Butler: Sexual Politics, Social Change and the Power of the Performative* (Oxford: Routledge, 2008), 137.

2   Slavoj Žižek, "Class Struggle or Postmodernism? Yes, Please!" in *Contingency, Hegemony, Universality: Contemporary Dialogues on the Left* (London: Verso, 2000), 132, n.30.

3   Susan Stryker, "Transgender History, Homonormativity, and Disciplinarity," *Radical History Review* 2008, no. 100: 147.

4   Eve Kosofsky Sedgwick, *Epistemology of the Closet* (Berkeley: University of California Press, 1990); David Halperin, *One Hundred Years of Homosexuality and Other Essays in Greek Love* (New York: Routledge, 1990).

5   David Halperin, "The Normalization of Queer Theory," *Journal of Homosexuality* 45, nos. 2–4 (2003), 340.

6   Michael Warner, *Publics and Counterpublics* (New York: Zone Books, 2002).

7   J. Jack Halberstam, *Gaga Feminism: Sex, Gender, and the End of Normal* (Boston: Beacon Press, 2012).

8   David Halperin, *Saint Foucault: Towards a Gay Hagiography* (Oxford: Oxford University Press, 1995), 62.

9   Glenn Burger, *Chaucer's Queer Nation* (Minneapolis: University of Minnesota Press, 2003), x.

10   Bill Burgwinkle, "Queer Theory and the Middle Ages," French Studies 60, no. 1, (January 2006), 82.

11   Madhavi Menon (ed.), *Shakesqueer: A Queer Companion to the Complete Works of Shakespeare* (Durham, NC: Duke University Press, 2011), 11.

MODULE 11
IMPACT AND INFLUENCE TODAY

KEY POINTS

- A quarter of a century after *Gender Trouble* was published it remains a landmark text for feminism,* gender* studies, and queer theory.*

- The core ideas of performativity* and social constructivism*—that we act out a gender until it becomes real, according to the rules of society—are alive and well everywhere from feminist and literary studies to terrorism and quantum physics.

- In literary studies Judith Butler's main ideas have been widely accepted and applied, but in feminism they remain the subject of fierce debate.

Position

Judith Butler's *Gender Trouble: Feminism and the Subversion of Identity* was published in 1990 but remains at the top of the reading list for anyone interested in feminism, gender, and sexuality. Concepts such as performativity (acting and therefore becoming a gender) and social constructivism (notions of reality created by society) are to be found everywhere, in a wide range of disciplines. This means that even where Butler's work is contested, it is never ignored.

Gender Trouble has become the touchstone text of performativity among literary critics. The sense in which Butler uses this term is particularly useful in a field where all subjectivity* (or "personhood") must be formed through language. Performativity and social constructivism are literary ways of reading the world,[1] they led to worldly ways of reading literary texts.[2]

> **❝**Butler's theories have generated as much hostility as adulation and, judging by a number of recent critiques and criticisms, it would seem that the debates arising from her work have by no means been 'resolved'.**❞**
>
> Sara Salih, *Judith Butler*

Butler is at the very center of debates within feminism and lesbian, gay, bisexual, and transsexual (LGBT*) politics. Her ideas continue to spark arguments about whether there are any "natural* facts" or whether everything simply comes down to "social constructions." Prominent feminists such as Martha Nussbaum* and Toril Moi* prefer a less radical version of the constructivist argument, and this guarantees sometimes ill-tempered debate with Butler.

Moi, for instance, has responded to Butler's work by stating that "we do not have to believe the word 'woman' always carries heavy metaphysical baggage." Feminists can, she says, contrary to Butler's claims, think about the idea of what a woman is without falling into the trap of confirming women's lower place in society. Indeed, for Moi, "the question of what a woman is, is crucial to feminist theory, and ... anyone who is willing to think it through once more from the beginning stands to gain a real sense of intellectual freedom."[3]

Interaction

Butler's theories have had a smoother ride in literary studies than in feminist philosophy. Literary critics are used to dealing in what Paul Strohm* calls "practical theory." This is a "voluntarily 'impure' theory: project oriented, aimed at explaining the text, rather than its own vindication."[4] Terms such as "sex" and "gender," as well as Butler's more specific "social fiction," "performativity," and "normativity" (expected and acceptable behavior), are extremely useful to critics. They do not need to question whether Butler's contentions are *true*, as long as they remain useful *for* the literary text.[5]

Gender Trouble also has a role in fields as diverse as terrorism studies and quantum physics. Queer theorist Jasbir Puar's* 2007 *Terrorist Assemblages* explores formerly marginalized identities in America through how their acceptance has been affected by historical change and questions of scale.[6] For Puar, the rights extended to lesbian, gay, bisexual, and transsexual (LBGT*) people in America led to a new identity politics. Minorities are allowed to share in acting out a national identity made stable by tolerating such difference.[7] This "homonationalism"* builds on Butler's work by examining socially acceptable behavior at the national level. For example, gay families are allowed as long as they resemble straight families. And everyone must share the accepted set of American values.

Karen Barad's* work uses physics to restage the debate over natural facts versus social fictions. As a feminist theoretical physicist, she sees performativity not as an "invitation to turn everything (including material bodies) into words," but as "a contestation of the unexamined habits of mind that grant language and other powers of representation more power in determining our ontologies* than they deserve."[8] Her 2007 book *Meeting the Universe Halfway* is possibly the most significant contribution to the debate on social constructivism (society's ability to create what we accept as "reality") since *Gender Trouble* itself.[9]

The Continuing Debate

Gender Trouble continues to fuel considerable debate within the feminist movement, often driven by an abiding dislike for Butler's ideas among some eminent critics. For them, Butler is undermining the fight for female equality.

Feminists following in Butler's footsteps run the risk of neglecting feminist aims altogether, according to Moi. In the essay *What is a Woman?* she suggests that Butler's discussion of sex itself as culturally constructed is "unpromising" as a starting point for a liberation politics. It is a diversion from the real project of feminism. The "new theoretical problems that poststructuralists feel compelled to resolve," she states, "no longer have any connection with bodies, sex, or gender."[10] For this reason their work is "plagued by internal contradictions, mired in unnecessary philosophical and theoretical elaborations."[11]

Nussbaum's critique is also aimed at Butler and her followers. As a supporter of political and legal intervention on women's behalf, Nussbaum defends the need for generally agreed norms in society—the very idea Butler questions in *Gender Trouble*. Her most famous attack on Butler was "The Professor of Parody,"[12] but she also wrote a more general critique in "Women and Cultural Universals," an essay in her book *Sex and Social Justice*. Although she never actually names Butler, the essay shares unflattering anecdotes in which "anti-universalists" take up "positions that converge ... with the positions of reaction, oppression, and sexism."[13] The questions Nussbaum raises remain to be answered.

NOTES

1   See the argument presented in chapters 2 and 4 of David Simpson, *The Academic Postmodern and the Rule of Literature: A Report on Half Knowledge* (Chicago: University of Chicago Press, 1996).

2   See Jonathon Culler, "The Literary in Theory," in *What's Left of Theory? New Work on the Politics of Literary Theory*, ed. Judith Butler, John Guillory and Kendall Thomas (London: Routledge, 2000), 282–3.

3   Toril Moi, *What is a Woman? and Other Essays* (Oxford: Oxford University Press, 1999), 10.

4   Paul Strohm, *Theory and the Premodern Text* (Minneapolis: University of Minnesota Press, 2000).

5   An exemplary instance of such productive readings, leaning heavily on Butler, is Nicola McDonald's work on medieval romance. See e.g. her chapter "Gender" in *A Handbook of Middle English Studies*, ed. Marion Turner (Chichester: Wiley-Blackwell, 2013).

6   Jasbir Puar, *Terrorist Assemblages: Homonationalism in Queer Times* (Durham, NC: Duke University Press, 2007).

7   See also Maya Mikdashi, "Gay Rights as Human Rights: Pinkwashing Homonationalism", accessed July 5 2015, http://www.jadaliyya.com/pages/index/3560/gay-rights-as-human-rights_pinkwashing-homonationa.

8   Karen Barad, "Posthumanist Performativity: Toward an Understanding of How Matter Comes to Matter," *Signs: Journal of Women in Culture and Society* 28, no. 3 (2003).

9   Karen Barad, *Meeting the Universe Halfway: Quantum Physics and the Entanglement of Matter and Meaning* (Durham, NC: Duke University Press, 2007).

10 Moi, *What is a Woman*, 31.

11 Moi, *What is a Woman*, 59.

12 Martha C. Nussbaum, "The Professor of Parody", in *Philosophical Interventions: Reviews, 1986–2011* (Oxford: Oxford University Press, 2012), 203.

13 Martha C. Nussbaum, *Sex and Social Justice* (Oxford: Oxford University Press, 1999), 35–7.

MODULE 12
WHERE NEXT?

KEY POINTS

- While *Gender Trouble* has a secure reputation as a seminal text, developments in transsexual* politics and scholarship may make some of Judith Butler's theories seem dated.

- The book has an enduring value in debates on identity— it provides a vocabulary for tackling the essence of the human condition.

- As the key interdisciplinary text of the 1990s, the intellectual stature of *Gender Trouble* is unquestioned: few texts have been used so frequently in so many different disciplines by so many people.

Potential

Gender Trouble: Feminism and the Subversion of Identity seems certain to remain on the essential reading list for anyone involved in feminist theory and literary criticism. Students in both fields will continue to study Judith Butler's revolutionary ideas and find their own ways to respond.

The claims *Gender Trouble* makes and the language it uses to convey radical ideas will inform fresh debates and new analyses in a vast range of critical and theoretical texts. A quarter of a century after it appeared, *Gender Trouble* has become part of the cultural landscape. The book serves as a reference point for influential intellectuals around the world—whether they love it or hate it.

That said, the school of "strong social constructivism"* that took on Butler's idea of the body shaped by society is on the wane. The

❝Some trans people thought that in claiming that gender is performative that I was saying that it is all a fiction, and that a person's felt sense of gender was therefore "unreal." That was never my intention. I sought to expand our sense of what gender realities could be. But I think I needed to pay more attention to what people feel, how the primary experience of the body is registered, and the quite urgent and legitimate demand to have those aspects of sex recognized and supported. ❞

Judith Butler, Interview in *TransAdvocate*

growth of transgender* perspectives both inside and outside the academic world brings new ways of thinking about the relationships between sex, sexuality, gender, and the body. If sex is a product of how we are expected to act, what does it mean to be "trapped in the wrong body"? As the work of thinkers such as the feminist* philosophers Elizabeth Grosz* and Moira Gatens* shows, there is much to be done. They call for new ways to understand the body and sex that do not reject the reality of biological difference or fall back into biological determinism* (that is, that just being male or female externally makes a person *really* male or female).[1]

Future Directions

The leading queer theorists Jasbir Puar* and Karen Barad* highlight Butler's work as a rich source of insight for scholars across an array of fields. Now that *Gender Trouble* has been translated into many other languages, the number of researchers and theorists able to build on Butler's ideas can only grow. Moreover, as Gill Jagger* points out, the shifting realities of gendered and transgendered life across the world will only bring more debates about Butler's theories.[2]

Butler continues to be relevant to queer theory and the politics of sexual minorities—but *Gender Trouble*'s future also lies in challenging a broader audience. One important figure in taking Butler to new readers is Judith/Jack Halberstam.* Halberstam is a leading contemporary queer theorist and director of the Center for Feminist Research at the University of Southern California. She works to popularize queer theory while keeping its sophistication and critical powers. Using the term "low theory," she answers Butler's call to avoid "binary formulations" and searches for "different ways of being" that reach out to a broader community than just academics.[3] Her chosen "texts" range from avant-garde performance to Hollywood romantic comedies, by way of the cartoon *Spongebob Squarepants* and the pop star Lady Gaga. Halberstam is at the forefront of the field Butler helped to found. Her determination to reach out beyond the academic world is a vital contribution to the future of queer theory and the wider debate on gender and identity ignited by *Gender Trouble*.

Summary

Even when it is the subject of raging debate, *Gender Trouble*'s international status as an epoch-making text in philosophy, feminism, literary theory, and sociology is never in doubt. Butler makes a convincing argument for taking a completely new look at some of the most basic tenets of social reality.

Her book has stood the test of time and continues to shake up—trouble—everything a new reader assumes about who we really are. The book has been accused by opponents of undoing the very foundations of feminism as a political movement. However, it has done more to stimulate academic and public debate about the identity of women and sexual minorities than any text since the French thinker Simone de Beauvoir's* *The Second Sex*.

By putting forward a compelling argument for gender—and even sex—being created by society, *Gender Trouble* caused a sea change in identity politics. Butler forced readers to rethink many of their assumptions from the ground up. Her arguments stretched far beyond academic circles, into the wider world of feminist and LBGT* movements and left indelible marks on their activism.

Whether or not Butler's arguments completely convince the reader, the core concepts of *Gender Trouble* have become powerful tools for thinking about writing (in all its guises), the self, and the world. Enshrined now at the heart of so much work in the humanities and social sciences, Butler's concepts will ensure *Gender Trouble*'s status as a seminal work for years to come. Whether readers are won over by it or violently object to it, few are able to see the world in quite the same light again.

NOTES

1   See Elizabeth Grosz, *Volatile Bodies: Towards a Corporeal Feminism* (Bloomington, IN: Indiana University Press, 1994);

2   Gill Jagger, *Judith Butler: Sexual Politics, Social Change and the Power of the Performative* (Oxford: Routledge, 2008), 137–9.

3   Judith Halberstam, *The Queer Art of Failure* (Durham, NC: Duke University Press, 2011), 2.

GLOSSARY

GLOSSARY OF TERMS

Agency: philosophical term for the capacity to act with free will.

AIDS: acronym standing for acquired immune deficiency syndrome, caused by the human immunodeficiency virus (HIV), a disease that attacks sufferers' ability to fight off infections. During the 1980s it spread rapidly through gay communities in the US, leading to the "AIDS crisis."

Anthropology: the study of humans and human culture.

Anti-foundationalism: a philosophical term for a type of thinking that rejects the belief that there is some fundamental belief or principle that is the basic ground or foundation of inquiry and knowledge

Anti-semitism: racial and religious prejudice against Jews and Judaism.

BDSM: acronym standing for the sexual practices involving bondage, domination, sadism (pleasure from causing pain) and masochism (pleasure from receiving pain).

Binary: an either/or distinction in which no other options or categories exist.

Bisexuality: sexual orientation in which individuals are attracted to both male and female partners.

Close-reading: a range of literary critical practices characterized by offering close attention to texts themselves, rather than their author's intentions or other contextual information.

Compulsory heterosexuality: a regime of law and cultural assumptions that serve to make male–female attraction the dominant and "normal" form of sexuality.

Continental philosophy: a set of nineteenth- and twentieth-century philosophical traditions from Europe, often characterized by interest in language, subjectivity, and lived experience.

Determinism/deterministic: term for any mode of thought that sees events or conditions as caused/determined by other events or conditions in a way that could have no other possible outcome.

Dialectics: a philosophical term for a range of variant systems of thought (for example, Hegelian or Marxist dialectics) that work by taking two opposed concepts/theses and using the opposition to generate a third concept/thesis. It can be used as an argumentative or reasoning methodology, or, as in Hegel and Marx, as a fundamental principle for the development of reality itself.

Discourse/discursive: a philosophical term for the total system of ideas, attitudes, courses of action, beliefs, practices, and languages belonging to a given culture at a given point in time. Discursive practices or creations are those that belong to or arise from discourse—a word that is often used as nearly synonymous with "culture."

Early Modern: roughly, the time between the Middle Ages and the late eighteenth century.

Epistemology: the branch of philosophy concerned with the study of knowledge; questioning what can be known, how, and how conclusions can be reached.

Equal Rights Amendment: a proposed amendment to the United States Constitution guaranteeing equal rights for women. Introduced in Congress in 1923, it has yet to receive the necessary 38 state ratifications to enter into law.

Essentialism: a philosophical view in which any specific object of knowledge (for example, a person, a physical object, or a concept) is seen as having a set of attributes necessary to its identity.

Ethics: the branch of philosophy concerned with concepts of right and wrong conduct (also called moral philosophy).

Existentialism: a philosophical tradition associated with French philosophers Jean-Paul Sartre, Albert Camus, and Simone de Beauvoir. Existentialism takes the individual human as the starting point for thinking, and the source of meaning in the world.

Fanzine: a low-circulation magazine made by a fan of a particular person or movement—most commonly associated with musical subcultures such as punk and hardcore, from the mid-1970s onwards.

Feminism: a set of movements and ideologies seeking to achieve equality for women.

Foundationalism: a term for philosophical theories of knowledge that rest on secure foundations of certainty, or beliefs that are considered to be universal and infallible.

French theory: label for the set of philosophical writers and thinkers (such as Roland Barthes, Jacques Derrida, Michel Foucault, and Julia Kristeva) who came to prominence in and beyond France from the 1960s onwards. It is often closely associated with structuralism and poststucturalism.

Gender: the binary (generally feminine/masculine) set of different behaviors or styles of acting commonly taken as "normal" for a given sex.

Hermeneutics: the theory and methodology of interpretation.

Heteronormativity: the presumption that people naturally conform to two complementary genders (masculine/feminine) belonging to two sexes (male/female); accompanied by the presumption that heterosexuality is normal, and all other sexualities deviant.

Heterosexuality: male–female sexual orientation.

Holocaust: the persecution, deportation, and organized mass murder of approximately six million Jews (and other minorities) from across Europe in countries occupied by Nazi Germany from 1935 to 1945. Called "Shoah" in Hebrew.

Homonationalism: term coined by Jasbir Puar for the rise of nationalism in American LBGT communities, and the use of American LBGT acceptance to promote a unified identity of a tolerant America.

Homophobia: prejudice against homosexuals.

Homosexuality: same-sex sexual orientation.

Identity politics: political arguments focusing on the interests of particular groups marked out as having a single identity.

Intersectionality: a term coined by Kimberlé Crenshaw for the study of the intersections between different forms of prejudice, domination, or oppression.

Israel–Palestine debate: the questions surrounding the political situation and contested territories of Israel and Palestine.

Judaism: monotheistic religion founded over 3,500 years ago in the Middle East. Today its practitioners, Jews, are largely concentrated in Israel and the United States, with smaller populations in dozens of other countries around the world.

Juridical: relating to the law.

Kinship: status of familial relation. Also a metaphorical sense of relatedness between humans.

LGBT: acronym standing for "lesbians, gays, bisexuals, and transsexuals," and referring to the set of movements supporting equal rights for these groups; currently, it is often lengthened LBGTIQ, to encompass intersex and queer individuals.

Medieval: the period of European history extending roughly from the year 500 to about 1500.

Morphology: in biology, this refers to the form and external characteristics of organisms; hence, sexual morphology refers to the external characteristics designated as male/female.

Natural: philosophically used by contrast with cultural or discursive. That is, belonging to nature rather than to human culture.

Nihilism: belief in nothing.

9/11: terrorist attack perpetrated on September 11, 2001, in which terrorists from the Islamic fundamentalist organization Al Qaeda crashed commercial jets into civilian and military targets in America, damaging the Pentagon in Washington, DC and destroying the World Trade Center (the Twin Towers) in New York.

Norm/normativity: expected patterns of behavior that also have the function of prescribing what is acceptable.

Ontology: the science or study of being or the nature of existing.

Patriarchy: social dominance by men.

Performativity: in gender studies, this refers to the idea that by acting as masculine or feminine, individuals do not just describe their masculinity or femininity, but actually bring it into being.

Phallogocentrism: a term coined by Jacques Derrida, combining "logocentrism", the deterministic belief in rationality's capacity to understand the world, and "phallocentrism", meaning masculine-gendered or patriarchal assumptions. It seeks to describe Western thought as inherently male-gendered.

Postmodernism: often strongly linked to poststructuralism, this term applies to schools of thought or art seeking to problematize standard assumptions and rules, forcing people to reconsider the foundations of their thought.

Poststructuralism: an anti-foundationalist philosophical school founded by the French philosopher Jacques Derrida. Skeptics have criticized it for destroying the basis of philosophical enquiry altogether.

Post-war era: the period immediately following on from World War II in Europe and America.

Pride movement: the international movement against LGBT discrimination.

Psychoanalysis: a set of theories for treating psychological illness, first elaborated by Austrian physician Sigmund Freud at the end of the nineteenth century.

Public sphere: an area in social life where individuals can come together to freely discuss and identify problems in society, and by doing so, influence political action.

Queer theory: a broad field of poststructuralist theory associated with both LBGT studies and women's studies, concerned with enquiry into both what is considered "normal" and supposedly deviant identity categories.

Quietism: an acceptance of the way things are, and a refusal to resist or to attempt to change them.

Reification: bringing into being or making real an abstract concept, such as gender categories.

Second-wave feminism: feminism of the post-war era, often strongly influenced by the French thinker Simone de Beauvoir, focused on issues such as women's sexual freedom, workplace equality, and reproductive rights.

Semiotics: the study of meaning, communication, and processes to do with linguistic signs.

Separatism: separation of a group of people from a larger body on the basis of ethnicity, religion, or gender.

Sex: the biological distinction between male and female.

Sexuality: the specific nature of our sexual desires.

Social constructivism: a philosophical viewpoint that regards perceptions of reality as constructed in and by discourse.

Structuralism: a foundationalist mode of thought that seeks to relate elements of culture to deep underlying structures, and to each other through such structures.

Subject: a philosophical term for the individual person.

Subject formation: a philosophical term for the ways in which "personhood" is produced.

Subjectivity: a philosophical term for the status of being a person, or "personhood"

Theory Wars: name given to a series of often heated academic debates during the 1980s and 1990s regarding the value of poststructuralist* theory in the humanities.

Transgender/trans/transsexual: having a gender identity or expression not matching one's assigned sex.

Utopia: term for a perfect society; coined by Sir Thomas More in his 1516 work *Utopia*.

World War II: a global war that occurred between 1939 and 1945.

PEOPLE MENTIONED IN THE TEXT

Karen Barad (b. 1956) is an American feminist theorist and physicist. She is currently professor of feminist studies, philosophy, and history of consciousness at the University of California, Santa Cruz.

Herculine Barbin (1838–1868) was a French intersex person, or hermaphrodite, whose memoirs were published initially in 1872, before being republished with an introduction by Michel Foucault in 1980.

Seyla Benhabib (b. 1950): is a Turkish American philosopher. Currently the Eugene Mayer Professor of Political Science and Philosophy at Yale University, she has published books on the philosophers Hannah Arendt and Jürgen Habermas.

Glenn Burger is a medievalist literary critic currently teaching at City University of New York.

Bill Burgwinkle is a professor in medieval French and Occitan literature at the University of Cambridge.

Geoffrey Chaucer (c. 1343–1400) was an English poet known as the father of English literature; best known for *The Canterbury Tales*.

Nancy Chodorow (b. 1944) is a feminist sociologist and psychoanalyst, whose major works include *The Reproduction of Mothering: Psychoanalysis and the Sociology of Gender* (1978), *Feminism and Psychoanalytic Theory* (1989), and *Femininities, Masculinities, Sexualities: Freud and Beyond* (1994).

Hélène Cixous (b. 1937) is an influential French feminist writer and philosopher, considered one of the mothers of poststructuralist feminist theory; widely known for her 1975 article "The Laugh of the Medusa," and her elaboration of the idea of *écriture feminine* ("feminine writing").

Kimberlé Crenshaw (b. 1959) is an American scholar and critical race theorist. A professor at the UCLA School of Law, she is best known for elaborating the concept of intersectionality.

Simone de Beauvoir (1908–1986) was a French feminist philosopher and writer known as the founder of second-wave feminism. The author of novels and essays, as well as philosophical studies, she remains best known for her 1949 feminist study *The Second Sex*.

Jacques Derrida (1930–2004) was a French philosopher known as the father of poststructuralism. Major works include *Of Grammatology* (1967; translated by Gayatri Spivak in 1976), and *Writing and Difference* (also 1967).

Lee Edelman (b. 1953) is an influential queer theorist and professor of English at Tufts University; best known for his 2004 book *No Future. Queer Theory and the Death Drive*

Michel Foucault (1926–1984) was a hugely influential French philosopher, historian and social theorist, whose work is a key influence on poststructuralism and queer theory. Highly prolific, his best-known works today include *Madness and Civilization* (1961), *The Order of Things* (1966), and *The History of Sexuality* (three volumes, 1976, 1984, 1984).

Carla Freccero (b. 1956) is a literary critic and feminist. She is currently professor and chair in literature and the history of consciousness, University of California, Santa Cruz.

Moira Gatens (b. 1954) is a feminist philosopher, currently Challis Professor of Philosophy at the University of Sydney.

Elizabeth Grosz (b. 1952) is a feminist philosopher and professor of women's studies at Duke University.

Jack/Judith Halberstam (b. 1961) is a queer theorist and cultural critic; currently professor of English and director of the Center for Feminist Research at the University of Southern California, she is best known for her books *Female Masculinity* (1998) and *The Queer Art of Failure* (2011).

David Halperin (b. 1952) is a queer theorist and critic, best known for his book *One Hundred Years of Homosexuality* (1990). He is currently professor of the history and theory of sexuality at the University of Michigan.

Georg Wilhelm Friedrich Hegel (1770–1831) was a German philosopher and a central influence on modern Continental philosophy; best known for his reformulation of dialectics. Among his many works, *The Phenomenology of Spirit* (1807) is perhaps the best known, and a classic account of subject formation.

Lynne Huffer (b. 1960) is an author and the Samuel Candler Dobbs Professor of Women's, Gender, and Sexuality Studies at Emory University. She has taught at Yale and Rice Universities, and her fields of study include feminist theory; queer theory; gay, lesbian, bisexual, and transgender studies; modern French and francophone literature; literary theory; and ethics.

Luce Irigaray (b. 1930) is a Belgian-born French feminist philosopher and psychoanalyst, best known for her works *Speculum of the Other Woman* (1974) and *This Sex Which Is Not One* (1977).

Gill Jagger is a lecturer in the department of Social Sciences at the University of Hull. Her research interests include poststructuralist theory and gender, sexual difference and the body and she is the author of *Judith Butler: Sexual Politics, Social Change and the Power of the Performative* (2008)

Franz Kafka (1883–1924) was a Jewish German-language novelist and writer of short stories who lived in Prague. He is best known for his complex parables of subjugated human existence, including *The Trial*, posthumously published in 1925.

Julia Kristeva (b. 1941) is a Bulgarian French feminist philosopher, literary critic and psychoanalyst. She is best known for her structuralist work on literature and linguistics, and above all for her elaboration of "intertextuality," in such books as *Desire in Language: A Semiotic Approach to Literature and Art* (1969).

Jacques Lacan (1901–1981) was a French psychoanalyst and philosopher whose work was highly influential in 1960s and 70s French thought. He is best known for his *Écrits* (1966).

Karl Marx (1818–1883) was a German philosopher, economist and revolutionary socialist known as the father of Communism. He is the co-author of *The Communist Manifesto* (1848) and author of *Capital* (1867–94).

Catharine McKinnon (b. 1946) is an American feminist, lawyer, and activist, known for her anti-pornography work and feminist activism; among her best-known work is *Feminism Unmodified: Discourses on Life and Law* (1987).

Toril Moi (b. 1953) is a Norwegian-born feminist theorist and literary critic. Currently the James B. Duke Professor of Literature and Romance Studies and professor of English, Philosophy and Theatre Studies at Duke University, she is best known for *What Is a Woman? And Other Essays* (1999).

Friedrich Nietzsche (1844–1900) was a German philosopher and classical scholar known for his literary style and radical questioning of received values; among his best-known works are *On Truth and Lies in a Nonmoral Sense* (1873) and *On the Genealogy of Morality* (1887).

Martha C. Nussbaum, (b. 1947) is an American philosopher and feminist known for her work on legal theory, feminism, and ethics. She is currently the Ernst Freund Distinguished Service Professor of Law and Ethics at the University of Chicago, and her works include *The Fragility of Goodness* (1986) and *Sex and Social Justice* (1998).

Jasbir Puar (b. 1967) is a queer theorist who currently teaches women's and gender studies at Rutgers University, and who is the author of *Terrorist Assemblages: Homonationalism in Queer Times* (2007).

Gayle Rubin (b. 1949) is an American cultural anthropologist and feminist activist, best known for her essay "The Traffic in Women: Notes on the 'Political Economy' of Sex" (1975). She is an associate professor of Anthropology and Women's Studies at the University of Michigan.

Jean-Paul Sartre (1905–1980) was a French existentialist philosopher, playwright and novelist; best known among philosophers for *Being and Nothingness* (1943).

Eve Kosofsky Sedgwick (1950–2009) was an American queer theorist and literary critic, best known for *Epistemology of the Closet* (1990).

Alan Sokal (b. 1955) is a physicist and mathematician who has become known as a critic of postmodernism and poststructuralism in the wake of his widely publicized hoaxing of the theory journal *Social Text* in 1996. He is best known for *Fashionable Nonsense: Postmodern Intellectuals' Abuse of Science* (1997), co-authored with Jean Bricmont.

Gayatri Chakravorty Spivak (b. 1942) is a literary theorist and feminist, widely seen as the mother of postcolonial studies. She is a professor at Columbia University, and is best known for her essay "Can the Subaltern Speak?" and for her translation of Derrida's *Of Grammatology.*

Paul Strohm (b. 1938) is a medievalist literary critic and theorist who teaches literature at the University of Columbia. Author of a number of studies on medieval literature, his best-known book is *Theory and the Premodern Text* (2000).

Michael Warner (b. 1958) is a literary critic and social theorist. He holds the position of the Seymour H. Knox Professor of English Literature and American Studies at Yale University, and wrote *The Trouble with Normal: Sex, Politics, and the Ethics of Queer Life* (1999) and *Publics and Counterpublics* (2002).

Monique Wittig (1935–2003) was a French author and lesbian feminist theorist whose work influenced second-wave feminism. She is best known for her 1978 essay "The Straight Mind."

Slavoj Žižek (b. 1949) is from Slovenia and is a famous Marxist philosopher, cultural critic, and author of over a dozen books on these subjects. He is currently a senior researcher at the Institute for Sociology and Philosophy at the University of Ljubljana in Slovenia, as well as the Global Distinguished Professor of German at New York University and international director of the Birkbeck Institute for the Humanities.

WORKS CITED

WORKS CITED

Barad, Karen. *Meeting the Universe Halfway: Quantum Physics and the Entanglement of Matter and Meaning*. Durham, NC: Duke University Press, 2007.

Belas, Oliver. "Performativity." In *The Encyclopedia of Literary and Cultural Theory*, edited by Gregory Castle, Robert Eaglestone, and M. Keith Booker. Oxford: Blackwell Publishing, 2011.

Benhabib, Seyla. "Feminism and Postmodernism: An Uneasy Alliance." In *Feminist Contentions: A Philosophical Exchange*, edited by Seyla Benhabib, 17–34. New York: Routledge, 1995.

Birkenstein, Cathy. "We Got the Wrong Gal: Rethinking the 'Bad' Academic Writing of Judith Butler." *College English* 72, no. 3 (January 2010): 269–83.

Blumenfeld, Warren J., and Margaret Sönser Breen. "Introduction." *International Journal of Sexuality and Gender Studies.* Special Issue: Butler Matters: Judith Butler's Impact on Feminist and Queer Studies since *Gender Trouble* 6, nos. 1–2 (April 2001): 1–5.

Bordo, Susan. "Postmodern Subjects, Postmodern Bodies." *Feminist Studies* 18, no. 1 (Spring 1992): 159–75.

Breen, Margaret Sönser, and Warren J. Blumenfeld (eds). *Butler Matters: Judith Butler's Impact on Feminist and Queer Studies*. Aldershot: Ashgate, 2005.

Burger, Glenn. *Chaucer's Queer Nation*. Minneapolis: University of Minnesota Press, 2003.

Burgwinkle, Bill. "Queer Theory and the Middle Ages." *French Studies* 60, no. 1, (January 2006): 82.

Butler, Judith. *Antigone's Claim: Kinship between Life and Death.* New York: Columbia University Press, 2000.

Bodies that Matter: On the Discursive Limits of "Sex". New York: Routledge, 1993.

"Contingent Foundations: Feminism and the Question of 'Postmodernism'." In *Feminist Contentions: A Philosophical Exchange*, edited by Seyla Benhabib. New York: Routledge, 1995.

Excitable Speech: A Politics of the Performative. New York and London: Routledge, 1997.

Frames of War: When is Life Grievable? London: Verso, 2009.

Gender Trouble: Feminism and the Subversion of Identity. New York: Routledge, 1999.

"Interview." *Haaretz*, February 24, 2010. Accessed June 5, 2015. http://www. haaretz.com/news/judith-butler-as-a-jew-i-was-taught-it-was-ethically-imperative-to-speak-up-1.266243

"Interview." *Lola Press Magazine*, May 2001. Accessed June 5, 2015. http:// www.lolapress.org/elec2/artenglish/butl_e.htm.

Parting Ways: Jewishness and the Critique of Zionism. New York: Columbia University Press, 2012.

Precarious Life: the Powers of Mourning and Violence. London: Verso, 2004.

The Psychic Life of Power: Theories in Subjection. Stanford, CA: Stanford University Press, 1997.

Subjects of Desire: Hegelian Reflections in Twentieth-Century France. New York: Columbia University Press, 1987.

Undoing Gender. New York: Routledge, 2004.

Carbin, Maria, and Sara Edenheim. "The Intersectional Turn in Feminist Theory: A Dream of a Common Language?" *European Journal of Women's Studies* 20, no. 3 (August 2013): 233–4.

Chodorow, Nancy. *The Reproduction of Mothering: Psychoanalysis and the Sociology of Gender.* Berkeley: University of California Press, 1978.

Cixous, Hélène. "The Laugh of the Medusa." Translated by Keith and Paula Cohen. *Signs* 1, no. 4 (Summer 1976): 875–93.

Crenshaw, Kimberlé. "Demarginalizing the Intersection of Race and Sex: A Black Feminist Critique of Antidiscrimination Doctrine, Feminist Theory and Antiracist Politics." *University of Chicago Legal Forum* (1989): 139–67.

Culler, Jonathon. "The Literary in Theory." In *What's Left of Theory? New Work on the Politics of Literary Theory*, edited by Judith Butler, John Guillory and Kendall Thomas, 282–3. London: Routledge, 2000.

Davis, Kathy. "Intersectionality as Buzzword: A Sociology of Science Perspective on What Makes a Feminist Theory Successful." *Feminist Theory* 9, no. 1 (April 2008): 67–85.

de Beauvoir, Simone. *The Second Sex.* Translated by E. M. Pashley. New York: Vintage, 1973.

Derrida, Jacques. *Writing and Difference.* Translated by Alan Bass. Abingdon: Routledge, 2001.

Dinshaw, Carolyn. *Getting Medieval: Sexualities and Communities, Pre- and Postmodern.* Durham, NC: Duke University Press, 1999.

Downing, Lisa, and Robert Gillett (eds). *Queer in Europe: Contemporary Case Studies*. Farnham: Ashgate, 2011.

Duggan, Lisa. "The Theory Wars, or, Who's Afraid of Judith Butler?" *Journal of Women's History* 10, no. 1 (1998): 9–19.

Foucault, Michel. *Discipline and Punish: The Birth of the Prison*. Translated by Alan Sheridan. Harmondsworth: Penguin, 1991.

The History of Sexuality. Translated by Robert Hurley. 3 volumes. Harmondsworth: Penguin, 1990.

Gatens, Moira. *Imaginary Bodies: Ethics, Power and Corporeality*. London: Routledge, 1996.

Grosz, Elizabeth. *Volatile Bodies: Toward a Corporeal Feminism*. Bloomington: Indiana University Press, 1994.

Halberstam, J. Jack. *Gaga Feminism: Sex, Gender, and the End of Normal* Boston: Beacon Press, 2012.

The Queer Art of Failure. Durham NC: Duke University Press, 2011.

Halperin, David M. *Saint Foucault: Towards a Gay Hagiography.* Oxford: Oxford University Press, 1995.

Irigaray, Luce. *Speculum of the Other Woman*. Translated by Gillian C. Gill. Ithaca, NY: Cornell University Press, 1985.

This Sex Which is Not One. Translated by Catherine Porter and Carolyn Burke. Ithaca, NY: Cornell University Press, 1985.

Jagger, Gill. *Judith Butler: Sexual Politics, Social Change and the Power of the Performative*. Routledge, 2008.

Johnston, Belinda. "Renaissance Body Matters: Judith Butler and the Sex that Is One." In *Butler Matters: Judith Butler's Impact on Feminist and Queer Studies*, edited by Margaret Sönser Breen and Warren J. Blumenfeld, 123–44. Aldershot: Ashgate, 2005.

Leitch, Vincent B., et al. (eds). *The Norton Anthology of Theory and Criticism*. New York: W. W. Norton and Company, 2001.

Lloyd, Moya. *Judith Butler: From Norms to Politics*. Cambridge: Polity Press, 2007.

MacKinnon, Catharine A. *Feminism Unmodified: Discourses on Life and Law*. Cambridge, MA: Harvard University Press, 1987.

Mayol, Pierre "Compte rendu: Judith Butler, *Trouble dans le genre: pour un feminisme de la subversion.*" *Agora* 41, no. 41 (2006): 142–63.

McDonald, Nicola. "Gender." In *A Handbook of Middle English Studies*, edited by Marion Turner. Chichester: Wiley-Blackwell, 2013.

Menon, Madhavi (ed.). *Shakesqueer: A Queer Companion to the Complete Works of Shakespeare*. Durham, NC: Duke University Press, 2011.

Mikdashi, Maya. "Gay Rights as Human Rights: Pinkwashing Homonationalism." Accessed July 5, 2015. http://www.jadaliyya.com/pages/index/3560/gay-rights-as-human-rights_pinkwashing-homonationa

Mitchell, Kaye. "Judith Butler." In *The Encyclopedia of Literary and Cultural Theory*, edited by Gregory Castle, Robert Eaglestone, and M. Keith Booker. Oxford: Blackwell Publishing, 2011.

Moi, Toril. *What is a Woman? and Other Essays*. Oxford: Oxford University Press, 1999.

Nash, Margaret. "Review: *Gender Trouble: Feminism and the Subversion of Identity* by Judith Butler; *Homophobia: A Weapon of Sexism* by Suzanne Pharr." *Hypatia* 5, no. 3 (Autumn 1990): 171–5.

Nussbaum, Martha C. "The Professor of Parody." In *Philosophical Interventions: Reviews, 1986–2011*. Oxford: Oxford University Press, 2012.

Sex and Social Justice. Oxford: Oxford University Press, 1999.

Puar, Jasbir. *Terrorist Assemblages: Homonationalism in Queer Times.* Durham, NC: Duke University Press, 2007.

Rubin, Gayle. "The Traffic in Women: Notes on the 'Political Economy' of Sex." In *Toward an Anthropology of Women*, edited by Rayna Reiter. New York, Monthly Review Press: 1975.

Salih, Sara. *Judith Butler*. London: Routledge, 2002.

Sedgwick, Eve. *Epistemology of the Closet.* Berkeley: University of California Press, 1990.

Simpson, David. *The Academic Postmodern and the Rule of Literature: A Report on Half Knowledge*. Chicago: University of Chicago Press, 1996.

Sokal, Alan, and Jean Bricmont. *Fashionable Nonsense: Postmodern Intellectuals' Abuse of Science*. New York: Picador, 1998.

Strohm, Paul. *Theory and the Premodern Text*. Minneapolis: University of Minnesota Press, 2000.

Stryker, Susan. "Transgender History, Homonormativity, and Disciplinarity." *Radical History Review* 2008, no. 100: 145–57.

Warner, Michael. *Publics and Counterpublics*. New York: Zone Books, 2002.

The Trouble with Normal: Sex, Politics, and the Ethics of Queer Life. New York: Free Press, 1999.

Weinthal, Benjamin, "Envoy to Germany: Awardee Ignores Terror on Israel." *Jewish Post*, August 28, 2012. Accessed June 5, 2015. http://www.jpost.com/Jewish-World/Jewish-News/Envoy-to-Germany-Awardee-ignores-terror-on-Israel.

Wittig, Monique. *The Straight Mind and Other Essays.* Boston: Beacon Press, 1992.

Žižek, Slavoj. "Class Struggle or Postmodernism? Yes, Please!" In *Contingency, Hegemony, Universality: Contemporary Dialogues on the Left*, Judith Butler, Ernesto Laclau, and Slavoj Žižek, 90–135. London: Verso, 2000

THE MACAT LIBRARY
BY DISCIPLINE

AFRICANA STUDIES

Chinua Achebe's *An Image of Africa: Racism in Conrad's Heart of Darkness*
W. E. B. Du Bois's *The Souls of Black Folk*
Zora Neale Huston's *Characteristics of Negro Expression*
Martin Luther King Jr's *Why We Can't Wait*
Toni Morrison's *Playing in the Dark: Whiteness in the American Literary Imagination*

ANTHROPOLOGY

Arjun Appadurai's *Modernity at Large: Cultural Dimensions of Globalisation*
Philippe Ariès's *Centuries of Childhood*
Franz Boas's *Race, Language and Culture*
Kim Chan & Renée Mauborgne's *Blue Ocean Strategy*
Jared Diamond's *Guns, Germs & Steel: the Fate of Human Societies*
Jared Diamond's *Collapse: How Societies Choose to Fail or Survive*
E. E. Evans-Pritchard's *Witchcraft, Oracles and Magic Among the Azande*
James Ferguson's *The Anti-Politics Machine*
Clifford Geertz's *The Interpretation of Cultures*
David Graeber's *Debt: the First 5000 Years*
Karen Ho's *Liquidated: An Ethnography of Wall Street*
Geert Hofstede's *Culture's Consequences: Comparing Values, Behaviors, Institutes and Organizations across Nations*
Claude Lévi-Strauss's *Structural Anthropology*
Jay Macleod's *Ain't No Makin' It: Aspirations and Attainment in a Low-Income Neighborhood*
Saba Mahmood's *The Politics of Piety: The Islamic Revival and the Feminist Subject*
Marcel Mauss's *The Gift*

BUSINESS

Jean Lave & Etienne Wenger's *Situated Learning*
Theodore Levitt's *Marketing Myopia*
Burton G. Malkiel's *A Random Walk Down Wall Street*
Douglas McGregor's *The Human Side of Enterprise*
Michael Porter's *Competitive Strategy: Creating and Sustaining Superior Performance*
John Kotter's *Leading Change*
C. K. Prahalad & Gary Hamel's *The Core Competence of the Corporation*

CRIMINOLOGY

Michelle Alexander's *The New Jim Crow: Mass Incarceration in the Age of Colorblindness*
Michael R. Gottfredson & Travis Hirschi's *A General Theory of Crime*
Richard Herrnstein & Charles A. Murray's *The Bell Curve: Intelligence and Class Structure in American Life*
Elizabeth Loftus's *Eyewitness Testimony*
Jay Macleod's *Ain't No Makin' It: Aspirations and Attainment In a Low-Income Neighborhood*
Philip Zimbardo's *The Lucifer Effect*

ECONOMICS

Janet Abu-Lughod's *Before European Hegemony*
Ha-Joon Chang's *Kicking Away the Ladder*
David Brion Davis's *The Problem of Slavery in the Age of Revolution*
Milton Friedman's *The Role of Monetary Policy*
Milton Friedman's *Capitalism and Freedom*
David Graeber's *Debt: the First 5000 Years*
Friedrich Hayek's *The Road to Serfdom*
Karen Ho's *Liquidated: An Ethnography of Wall Street*

The Macat Library By Discipline

John Maynard Keynes's *The General Theory of Employment, Interest and Money*
Charles P. Kindleberger's *Manias, Panics and Crashes*
Robert Lucas's *Why Doesn't Capital Flow from Rich to Poor Countries?*
Burton G. Malkiel's *A Random Walk Down Wall Street*
Thomas Robert Malthus's *An Essay on the Principle of Population*
Karl Marx's *Capital*
Thomas Piketty's *Capital in the Twenty-First Century*
Amartya Sen's *Development as Freedom*
Adam Smith's *The Wealth of Nations*
Nassim Nicholas Taleb's *The Black Swan: The Impact of the Highly Improbable*
Amos Tversky's & Daniel Kahneman's *Judgment under Uncertainty: Heuristics and Biases*
Mahbub Ul Haq's *Reflections on Human Development*
Max Weber's *The Protestant Ethic and the Spirit of Capitalism*

FEMINISM AND GENDER STUDIES

Judith Butler's *Gender Trouble*
Simone De Beauvoir's *The Second Sex*
Michel Foucault's *History of Sexuality*
Betty Friedan's *The Feminine Mystique*
Saba Mahmood's *The Politics of Piety: The Islamic Revival and the Feminist Subjec*t
Joan Wallach Scott's *Gender and the Politics of History*
Mary Wollstonecraft's *A Vindication of the Rights of Woman*
Virginia Woolf's *A Room of One's Own*

GEOGRAPHY

The Brundtland Report's *Our Common Future*
Rachel Carson's *Silent Spring*
Charles Darwin's *On the Origin of Species*
James Ferguson's *The Anti-Politics Machine*
Jane Jacobs's *The Death and Life of Great American Cities*
James Lovelock's *Gaia: A New Look at Life on Earth*
Amartya Sen's *Development as Freedom*
Mathis Wackernagel & William Rees's *Our Ecological Footprint*

HISTORY

Janet Abu-Lughod's *Before European Hegemony*
Benedict Anderson's *Imagined Communities*
Bernard Bailyn's *The Ideological Origins of the American Revolution*
Hanna Batatu's *The Old Social Classes And The Revolutionary Movements Of Iraq*
Christopher Browning's *Ordinary Men: Reserve Police Battalion 101 and the Final Solution in Poland*
Edmund Burke's *Reflections on the Revolution in France*
William Cronon's *Nature's Metropolis: Chicago And The Great West*
Alfred W. Crosby's *The Columbian Exchange*
Hamid Dabashi's *Iran: A People Interrupted*
David Brion Davis's *The Problem of Slavery in the Age of Revolution*
Nathalie Zemon Davis's *The Return of Martin Guerre*
Jared Diamond's *Guns, Germs & Steel: the Fate of Human Societies*
Frank Dikotter's *Mao's Great Famine*
John W Dower's *War Without Mercy: Race And Power In The Pacific War*
W. E. B. Du Bois's *The Souls of Black Folk*
Richard J. Evans's *In Defence of History*
Lucien Febvre's *The Problem of Unbelief in the 16th Century*
Sheila Fitzpatrick's *Everyday Stalinism*

Eric Foner's *Reconstruction: America's Unfinished Revolution, 1863-1877*
Michel Foucault's *Discipline and Punish*
Michel Foucault's *History of Sexuality*
Francis Fukuyama's *The End of History and the Last Man*
John Lewis Gaddis's *We Now Know: Rethinking Cold War History*
Ernest Gellner's *Nations and Nationalism*
Eugene Genovese's *Roll, Jordan, Roll: The World the Slaves Made*
Carlo Ginzburg's *The Night Battles*
Daniel Goldhagen's *Hitler's Willing Executioners*
Jack Goldstone's *Revolution and Rebellion in the Early Modern World*
Antonio Gramsci's *The Prison Notebooks*
Alexander Hamilton, John Jay & James Madison's *The Federalist Papers*
Christopher Hill's *The World Turned Upside Down*
Carole Hillenbrand's *The Crusades: Islamic Perspectives*
Thomas Hobbes's *Leviathan*
Eric Hobsbawm's *The Age Of Revolution*
John A. Hobson's *Imperialism: A Study*
Albert Hourani's *History of the Arab Peoples*
Samuel P. Huntington's *The Clash of Civilizations and the Remaking of World Order*
C. L. R. James's *The Black Jacobins*
Tony Judt's *Postwar: A History of Europe Since 1945*
Ernst Kantorowicz's *The King's Two Bodies: A Study in Medieval Political Theology*
Paul Kennedy's *The Rise and Fall of the Great Powers*
Ian Kershaw's *The "Hitler Myth": Image and Reality in the Third Reich*
John Maynard Keynes's *The General Theory of Employment, Interest and Money*
Charles P. Kindleberger's *Manias, Panics and Crashes*
Martin Luther King Jr's *Why We Can't Wait*
Henry Kissinger's *World Order: Reflections on the Character of Nations and the Course of History*
Thomas Kuhn's *The Structure of Scientific Revolutions*
Georges Lefebvre's *The Coming of the French Revolution*
John Locke's *Two Treatises of Government*
Niccolò Machiavelli's *The Prince*
Thomas Robert Malthus's *An Essay on the Principle of Population*
Mahmood Mamdani's *Citizen and Subject: Contemporary Africa And The Legacy Of Late Colonialism*
Karl Marx's *Capital*
Stanley Milgram's *Obedience to Authority*
John Stuart Mill's *On Liberty*
Thomas Paine's *Common Sense*
Thomas Paine's *Rights of Man*
Geoffrey Parker's *Global Crisis: War, Climate Change and Catastrophe in the Seventeenth Century*
Jonathan Riley-Smith's *The First Crusade and the Idea of Crusading*
Jean-Jacques Rousseau's *The Social Contract*
Joan Wallach Scott's *Gender and the Politics of History*
Theda Skocpol's *States and Social Revolutions*
Adam Smith's *The Wealth of Nations*
Timothy Snyder's *Bloodlands: Europe Between Hitler and Stalin*
Sun Tzu's *The Art of War*
Keith Thomas's *Religion and the Decline of Magic*
Thucydides's *The History of the Peloponnesian War*
Frederick Jackson Turner's *The Significance of the Frontier in American History*
Odd Arne Westad's *The Global Cold War: Third World Interventions And The Making Of Our Times*

The Macat Library By Discipline

LITERATURE

Chinua Achebe's *An Image of Africa: Racism in Conrad's Heart of Darkness*
Roland Barthes's *Mythologies*
Homi K. Bhabha's *The Location of Culture*
Judith Butler's *Gender Trouble*
Simone De Beauvoir's *The Second Sex*
Ferdinand De Saussure's *Course in General Linguistics*
T. S. Eliot's *The Sacred Wood: Essays on Poetry and Criticism*
Zora Neale Huston's *Characteristics of Negro Expression*
Toni Morrison's *Playing in the Dark: Whiteness in the American Literary Imagination*
Edward Said's *Orientalism*
Gayatri Chakravorty Spivak's *Can the Subaltern Speak?*
Mary Wollstonecraft's *A Vindication of the Rights of Women*
Virginia Woolf's *A Room of One's Own*

PHILOSOPHY

Elizabeth Anscombe's *Modern Moral Philosophy*
Hannah Arendt's *The Human Condition*
Aristotle's *Metaphysics*
Aristotle's *Nicomachean Ethics*
Edmund Gettier's *Is Justified True Belief Knowledge?*
Georg Wilhelm Friedrich Hegel's *Phenomenology of Spirit*
David Hume's *Dialogues Concerning Natural Religion*
David Hume's *The Enquiry for Human Understanding*
Immanuel Kant's *Religion within the Boundaries of Mere Reason*
Immanuel Kant's *Critique of Pure Reason*
Søren Kierkegaard's *The Sickness Unto Death*
Søren Kierkegaard's *Fear and Trembling*
C. S. Lewis's *The Abolition of Man*
Alasdair MacIntyre's *After Virtue*
Marcus Aurelius's *Meditations*
Friedrich Nietzsche's *On the Genealogy of Morality*
Friedrich Nietzsche's *Beyond Good and Evil*
Plato's *Republic*
Plato's *Symposium*
Jean-Jacques Rousseau's *The Social Contract*
Gilbert Ryle's *The Concept of Mind*
Baruch Spinoza's *Ethics*
Sun Tzu's *The Art of War*
Ludwig Wittgenstein's *Philosophical Investigations*

POLITICS

Benedict Anderson's *Imagined Communities*
Aristotle's *Politics*
Bernard Bailyn's *The Ideological Origins of the American Revolution*
Edmund Burke's *Reflections on the Revolution in France*
John C. Calhoun's *A Disquisition on Government*
Ha-Joon Chang's *Kicking Away the Ladder*
Hamid Dabashi's *Iran: A People Interrupted*
Hamid Dabashi's *Theology of Discontent: The Ideological Foundation of the Islamic Revolution in Iran*
Robert Dahl's *Democracy and its Critics*
Robert Dahl's *Who Governs?*
David Brion Davis's *The Problem of Slavery in the Age of Revolution*

Alexis De Tocqueville's *Democracy in America*
James Ferguson's *The Anti-Politics Machine*
Frank Dikotter's *Mao's Great Famine*
Sheila Fitzpatrick's *Everyday Stalinism*
Eric Foner's *Reconstruction: America's Unfinished Revolution, 1863-1877*
Milton Friedman's *Capitalism and Freedom*
Francis Fukuyama's *The End of History and the Last Man*
John Lewis Gaddis's *We Now Know: Rethinking Cold War History*
Ernest Gellner's *Nations and Nationalism*
David Graeber's *Debt: the First 5000 Years*
Antonio Gramsci's *The Prison Notebooks*
Alexander Hamilton, John Jay & James Madison's *The Federalist Papers*
Friedrich Hayek's *The Road to Serfdom*
Christopher Hill's *The World Turned Upside Down*
Thomas Hobbes's *Leviathan*
John A. Hobson's *Imperialism: A Study*
Samuel P. Huntington's *The Clash of Civilizations and the Remaking of World Order*
Tony Judt's *Postwar: A History of Europe Since 1945*
David C. Kang's *China Rising: Peace, Power and Order in East Asia*
Paul Kennedy's *The Rise and Fall of Great Powers*
Robert Keohane's *After Hegemony*
Martin Luther King Jr.'s *Why We Can't Wait*
Henry Kissinger's *World Order: Reflections on the Character of Nations and the Course of History*
John Locke's *Two Treatises of Government*
Niccolò Machiavelli's *The Prince*
Thomas Robert Malthus's *An Essay on the Principle of Population*
Mahmood Mamdani's *Citizen and Subject: Contemporary Africa And The Legacy Of Late Colonialism*
Karl Marx's *Capital*
John Stuart Mill's *On Liberty*
John Stuart Mill's *Utilitarianism*
Hans Morgenthau's *Politics Among Nations*
Thomas Paine's *Common Sense*
Thomas Paine's *Rights of Man*
Thomas Piketty's *Capital in the Twenty-First Century*
Robert D. Putman's *Bowling Alone*
John Rawls's *Theory of Justice*
Jean-Jacques Rousseau's *The Social Contract*
Theda Skocpol's *States and Social Revolutions*
Adam Smith's *The Wealth of Nations*
Sun Tzu's *The Art of War*
Henry David Thoreau's *Civil Disobedience*
Thucydides's *The History of the Peloponnesian War*
Kenneth Waltz's *Theory of International Politics*
Max Weber's *Politics as a Vocation*
Odd Arne Westad's *The Global Cold War: Third World Interventions And The Making Of Our Times*

POSTCOLONIAL STUDIES

Roland Barthes's *Mythologies*
Frantz Fanon's *Black Skin, White Masks*
Homi K. Bhabha's *The Location of Culture*
Gustavo Gutiérrez's *A Theology of Liberation*
Edward Said's *Orientalism*
Gayatri Chakravorty Spivak's *Can the Subaltern Speak?*

The Macat Library By Discipline

PSYCHOLOGY

Gordon Allport's *The Nature of Prejudice*
Alan Baddeley & Graham Hitch's *Aggression: A Social Learning Analysis*
Albert Bandura's *Aggression: A Social Learning Analysis*
Leon Festinger's *A Theory of Cognitive Dissonance*
Sigmund Freud's *The Interpretation of Dreams*
Betty Friedan's *The Feminine Mystique*
Michael R. Gottfredson & Travis Hirschi's *A General Theory of Crime*
Eric Hoffer's *The True Believer: Thoughts on the Nature of Mass Movements*
William James's *Principles of Psychology*
Elizabeth Loftus's *Eyewitness Testimony*
A. H. Maslow's *A Theory of Human Motivation*
Stanley Milgram's *Obedience to Authority*
Steven Pinker's *The Better Angels of Our Nature*
Oliver Sacks's *The Man Who Mistook His Wife For a Hat*
Richard Thaler & Cass Sunstein's *Nudge: Improving Decisions About Health, Wealth and Happiness*
Amos Tversky's *Judgment under Uncertainty: Heuristics and Biases*
Philip Zimbardo's *The Lucifer Effect*

SCIENCE

Rachel Carson's *Silent Spring*
William Cronon's *Nature's Metropolis: Chicago And The Great West*
Alfred W. Crosby's *The Columbian Exchange*
Charles Darwin's *On the Origin of Species*
Richard Dawkin's *The Selfish Gene*
Thomas Kuhn's *The Structure of Scientific Revolutions*
Geoffrey Parker's *Global Crisis: War, Climate Change and Catastrophe in the Seventeenth Century*
Mathis Wackernagel & William Rees's *Our Ecological Footprint*

SOCIOLOGY

Michelle Alexander's *The New Jim Crow: Mass Incarceration in the Age of Colorblindness*
Gordon Allport's *The Nature of Prejudice*
Albert Bandura's *Aggression: A Social Learning Analysis*
Hanna Batatu's *The Old Social Classes And The Revolutionary Movements Of Iraq*
Ha-Joon Chang's *Kicking Away the Ladder*
W. E. B. Du Bois's *The Souls of Black Folk*
Émile Durkheim's *On Suicide*
Frantz Fanon's *Black Skin, White Masks*
Frantz Fanon's *The Wretched of the Earth*
Eric Foner's *Reconstruction: America's Unfinished Revolution, 1863-1877*
Eugene Genovese's *Roll, Jordan, Roll: The World the Slaves Made*
Jack Goldstone's *Revolution and Rebellion in the Early Modern World*
Antonio Gramsci's *The Prison Notebooks*
Richard Herrnstein & Charles A Murray's *The Bell Curve: Intelligence and Class Structure in American Life*
Eric Hoffer's *The True Believer: Thoughts on the Nature of Mass Movements*
Jane Jacobs's *The Death and Life of Great American Cities*
Robert Lucas's *Why Doesn't Capital Flow from Rich to Poor Countries?*
Jay Macleod's *Ain't No Makin' It: Aspirations and Attainment in a Low Income Neighborhood*
Elaine May's *Homeward Bound: American Families in the Cold War Era*
Douglas McGregor's *The Human Side of Enterprise*
C. Wright Mills's *The Sociological Imagination*

Thomas Piketty's *Capital in the Twenty-First Century*
Robert D. Putman's *Bowling Alone*
David Riesman's *The Lonely Crowd: A Study of the Changing American Character*
Edward Said's *Orientalism*
Joan Wallach Scott's *Gender and the Politics of History*
Theda Skocpol's *States and Social Revolutions*
Max Weber's *The Protestant Ethic and the Spirit of Capitalism*

THEOLOGY

Augustine's *Confessions*
Benedict's *Rule of St Benedict*
Gustavo Gutiérrez's *A Theology of Liberation*
Carole Hillenbrand's *The Crusades: Islamic Perspectives*
David Hume's *Dialogues Concerning Natural Religion*
Immanuel Kant's *Religion within the Boundaries of Mere Reason*
Ernst Kantorowicz's *The King's Two Bodies: A Study in Medieval Political Theology*
Søren Kierkegaard's *The Sickness Unto Death*
C. S. Lewis's *The Abolition of Man*
Saba Mahmood's *The Politics of Piety: The Islamic Revival and the Feminist Subject*
Baruch Spinoza's *Ethics*
Keith Thomas's *Religion and the Decline of Magic*

COMING SOON

Chris Argyris's *The Individual and the Organisation*
Seyla Benhabib's *The Rights of Others*
Walter Benjamin's *The Work Of Art in the Age of Mechanical Reproduction*
John Berger's *Ways of Seeing*
Pierre Bourdieu's *Outline of a Theory of Practice*
Mary Douglas's *Purity and Danger*
Roland Dworkin's *Taking Rights Seriously*
James G. March's *Exploration and Exploitation in Organisational Learning*
Ikujiro Nonaka's *A Dynamic Theory of Organizational Knowledge Creation*
Griselda Pollock's *Vision and Difference*
Amartya Sen's *Inequality Re-Examined*
Susan Sontag's *On Photography*
Yasser Tabbaa's *The Transformation of Islamic Art*
Ludwig von Mises's *Theory of Money and Credit*

Macat Disciplines

Access the greatest ideas and thinkers across entire disciplines, including

INEQUALITY

Ha-Joon Chang's, *Kicking Away the Ladder*

David Graeber's, *Debt: The First 5000 Years*

Robert E. Lucas's, *Why Doesn't Capital Flow from Rich To Poor Countries?*

Thomas Piketty's, *Capital in the Twenty-First Century*

Amartya Sen's, *Inequality Re-Examined*

Mahbub Ul Haq's, *Reflections on Human Development*

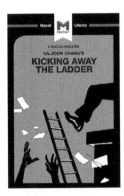

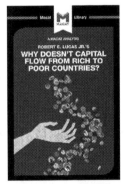

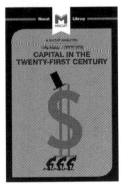

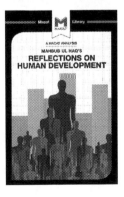

Macat analyses are available from all good bookshops and libraries.

Access hundreds of analyses through one, multimedia tool.

Join free for one month **library.macat.com**

Macat Disciplines

Access the greatest ideas and thinkers across entire disciplines, including

CRIMINOLOGY

Michelle Alexander's
The New Jim Crow: Mass Incarceration in the Age of Colorblindness

Michael R. Gottfredson & Travis Hirschi's
A General Theory of Crime

Elizabeth Loftus's
Eyewitness Testimony

Richard Herrnstein & Charles A. Murray's
The Bell Curve: Intelligence and Class Structure in American Life

Jay Macleod's
Ain't No Makin' It: Aspirations and Attainment in a Low-Income Neighborhood

Philip Zimbardo's
The Lucifer Effect

Macat analyses are available from all good bookshops and libraries.

Access hundreds of analyses through one, multimedia tool.
Join free for one month **library.macat.com**

Macat Disciplines

Access the greatest ideas and thinkers across entire disciplines, including

GLOBALIZATION

Arjun Appadurai's, *Modernity at Large: Cultural Dimensions of Globalisation*

James Ferguson's, *The Anti-Politics Machine*

Geert Hofstede's, *Culture's Consequences*

Amartya Sen's, *Development as Freedom*

Macat analyses are available from all good bookshops and libraries.

Access hundreds of analyses through one, multimedia tool.

Join free for one month **library.macat.com**

Macat Disciplines

Access the greatest ideas and thinkers across entire disciplines, including

Macat Disciplines

Access the greatest ideas and thinkers across entire disciplines, including

THE FUTURE OF DEMOCRACY

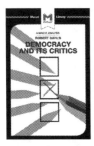

Robert A. Dahl's, *Democracy and Its Critics*
Robert A. Dahl's, *Who Governs?*
Alexis De Toqueville's, *Democracy In America*
Niccolò Machiavelli's, *The Prince*
John Stuart Mill's, *On Liberty*
Robert D. Putnam's, *Bowling Alone*
Jean-Jacques Rousseau's, *The Social Contract*
Henry David Thoreau's, *Civil Disobedience*

Macat Disciplines

Access the greatest ideas and thinkers across entire disciplines, including

TOTALITARIANISM

Sheila Fitzpatrick's, *Everyday Stalinism*
Ian Kershaw's, *The "Hitler Myth"*
Timothy Snyder's, *Bloodlands*

Macat Pairs

Analyse historical and modern issues from opposite sides of an argument. Pairs include:

INTERNATIONAL RELATIONS IN THE 21ST CENTURY

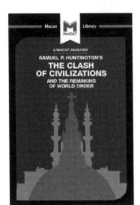

Samuel P. Huntington's
The Clash of Civilisations

In his highly influential 1996 book, Huntington offers a vision of a post-Cold War world in which conflict takes place not between competing ideologies but between cultures. The worst clash, he argues, will be between the Islamic world and the West: the West's arrogance and belief that its culture is a "gift" to the world will come into conflict with Islam's obstinacy and concern that its culture is under attack from a morally decadent "other."

Clash inspired much debate between different political schools of thought. But its greatest impact came in helping define American foreign policy in the wake of the 2001 terrorist attacks in New York and Washington.

Francis Fukuyama's
The End of History and the Last Man

Published in 1992, *The End of History and the Last Man* argues that capitalist democracy is the final destination for all societies. Fukuyama believed democracy triumphed during the Cold War because it lacks the fundamental contradictions" inherent in communism and satisfies our yearning for freedom and equality. Democracy therefore marks the endpoint in the evolution of ideology, and so the "end of history." There will still be "events," but no fundamental change in ideology.

Macat Disciplines

Access the greatest ideas and thinkers across entire disciplines, including

FEMINISM, GENDER AND QUEER STUDIES

Simone De Beauvoir's
The Second Sex

Michel Foucault's
History of Sexuality

Betty Friedan's
The Feminine Mystique

Saba Mahmood's
*The Politics of Piety:
The Islamic Revival and
the Feminist Subject*

Joan Wallach Scott's
*Gender and the
Politics of History*

Mary Wollstonecraft's
*A Vindication of the
Rights of Woman*

Virginia Woolf's
A Room of One's Own

Judith Butler's
Gender Trouble

 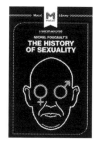  

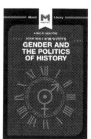   

Printed in the United States
by Baker & Taylor Publisher Services